An Analysis of

# Steven Pinker's

# The Better Angels of Our Nature
## Why Violence Has Declined

Joulia Smortchkova

www.macat.com
info@macat.com

Cover illustration: A. Richard Allen

*Cataloguing in Publication Data*
A catalogue record for this book is available from the British Library.
Library of Congress Cataloguing-in-Publication Data is available upon request.

ISBN 978-1-912303-65-6 (hardback)
ISBN 978-1-912128-21-1 (paperback)
ISBN 978-1-912282-53-1 (e-book)

**Notice**
The information in this book is designed to orientate readers of the work under analysis,
to elucidate and contextualise its key ideas and themes, and to aid in the development
of critical thinking skills. It is not meant to be used, nor should it be used, as a
substitute for original thinking or in place of original writing or research. References and
notes are provided for informational purposes and their presence does not constitute
endorsement of the information or opinions therein. This book is presented solely for
educational purposes. It is sold on the understanding that the publisher is not engaged
to provide any scholarly advice. The publisher has made every effort to ensure that
this book is accurate and up-to-date, but makes no warranties or representations with
regard to the completeness or reliability of the information it contains. The information
and the opinions provided herein are not guaranteed or warranted to produce particular
results and may not be suitable for students of every ability. The publisher shall not be
liable for any loss, damage or disruption arising from any errors or omissions, or from
the use of this book, including, but not limited to, special, incidental, consequential or
other damages caused, or alleged to have been caused, directly or indirectly, by the
information contained within.

# CONTENTS

## THE MACAT LIBRARY

The Macat Library is a series of unique academic explorations of seminal works in the humanities and social sciences – books and papers that have had a significant and widely recognised impact on their disciplines. It has been created to serve as much more than just a summary of what lies between the covers of a great book. It illuminates and explores the influences on, ideas of, and impact of that book. Our goal is to offer a learning resource that encourages critical thinking and fosters a better, deeper understanding of important ideas.

Each publication is divided into three Sections: Influences, Ideas, and Impact. Each Section has four Modules. These explore every important facet of the work, and the responses to it.

This Section-Module structure makes a Macat Library book easy to use, but it has another important feature. Because each Macat book is written to the same format, it is possible (and encouraged!) to cross-reference multiple Macat books along the same lines of inquiry or research. This allows the reader to open up interesting interdisciplinary pathways.

To further aid your reading, lists of glossary terms and people mentioned are included at the end of this book (these are indicated by an asterisk [*] throughout) – as well as a list of works cited.

Macat has worked with the University of Cambridge to identify the elements of critical thinking and understand the ways in which six different skills combine to enable effective thinking.
Three allow us to fully understand a problem; three more give us the tools to solve it. Together, these six skills make up the **PACIER** model of critical thinking. They are:

**ANALYSIS** – understanding how an argument is built
**EVALUATION** – exploring the strengths and weaknesses of an argument
**INTERPRETATION** – understanding issues of meaning

**CREATIVE THINKING** – coming up with new ideas and fresh connections
**PROBLEM-SOLVING** – producing strong solutions
**REASONING** – creating strong arguments

To find out more, visit **WWW.MACAT.COM.**

# CRITICAL THINKING AND *THE BETTER ANGELS OF OUR NATURE*

## Primary critical thinking skill: REASONING
## Secondary critical thinking skill: INTERPRETATION

Reasoning is the critical thinking skill concerned with the production of arguments: making them coherent, consistent, and well-supported; and responding to opposing positions where necessary. *The Better Angels of Our Nature* offers a step-by-step class in precisely these skills. Author Steven Pinker's central thesis is simple: mankind has become increasingly less violent over the centuries, and will continue to do so. Pinker is aware, though, that many people instinctively believe the opposite, and *Better Angels* is devoted to marshalling data to support and illustrate this central argument, as well as a series of secondary arguments about how and why humanity has become less violent. Pinker's interpretative skills – understanding the meaning of the complex evidence from history – are also on display throughout, as he tackles the ambiguities of his data, the problems it presents, and the viable inferences one can draw from it.

## ABOUT THE AUTHOR OF THE ORIGINAL WORK

**Steven Pinker** was a teenage anarchist. Today he is a world-renowned Harvard psychology professor, a best-selling author, and a leading cognitive scientist. Born in Canada in 1954, Pinker published his first best seller the year he turned 40. *The Language Instinct* explored the ideas of linguist Noam Chomsky and presented them to a popular audience. Pinker's reputation grew with his later books, including *How The Mind Works* and *The Blank Slate*. But it was in 2011, with the publication of *The Better Angels of Our Nature: Why Violence Has Declined*, that he began to be heralded as one of the most important global thinkers of our time.

## ABOUT THE AUTHOR OF THE ANALYSIS

**Dr Joulia Smortchkova** holds a PhD in social psychology from the Institut Jean Nicod (CNRS, ENS, EHESS), Paris. She is currently a Postdoctoral Fellow at the Ruhr-Universität Bochum.

## ABOUT MACAT

### GREAT WORKS FOR CRITICAL THINKING

Macat is focused on making the ideas of the world's great thinkers accessible and comprehensible to everybody, everywhere, in ways that promote the development of enhanced critical thinking skills.

It works with leading academics from the world's top universities to produce new analyses that focus on the ideas and the impact of the most influential works ever written across a wide variety of academic disciplines. Each of the works that sit at the heart of its growing library is an enduring example of great thinking. But by setting them in context – and looking at the influences that shaped their authors, as well as the responses they provoked – Macat encourages readers to look at these classics and game-changers with fresh eyes. Readers learn to think, engage and challenge their ideas, rather than simply accepting them.

"Macat offers an amazing first-of-its-kind tool for interdisciplinary learning and research. Its focus on works that transformed their disciplines and its rigorous approach, drawing on the world's leading experts and educational institutions, opens up a world-class education to anyone."

**Andreas Schleicher**
**Director for Education and Skills, Organisation for Economic**
**Co-operation and Development**

'Macat is taking on some of the major challenges in university education ... They have drawn together a strong team of active academics who are producing teaching materials that are novel in the breadth of their approach.'

**Prof Lord Broers,**
**former Vice-Chancellor of the University of Cambridge**

'The Macat vision is exceptionally exciting. It focuses upon new modes of learning which analyse and explain seminal texts which have profoundly influenced world thinking and so social and economic development. It promotes the kind of critical thinking which is essential for any society and economy.
This is the learning of the future.'

**Rt Hon Charles Clarke, former UK Secretary of State for Education**

'The Macat analyses provide immediate access to the critical conversation surrounding the books that have shaped their respective discipline, which will make them an invaluable resource to all of those, students and teachers, working in the field.'

**Professor William Tronzo, University of California at San Diego**

# WAYS IN TO THE TEXT

## KEY POINTS

- Born in 1954, Steven Pinker is a Canadian American professor of experimental psychology* at Harvard University and the author of many scholarly and popular books about language and human psychology. Experimental psychology is the study of the human mind and behavior in a way that is measurable and has a degree of scientific accuracy.

- *The Better Angels* argues that violence has declined over the course of human history, and explores the potential causes of that decline.

- Since its publication in 2011, *The Better Angels* has been widely regarded as one of the most controversial books about the history and psychology of violence.

### Who Is Steven Pinker?

Steven Arthur Pinker, the author of *The Better Angels of Our Nature: Why Violence Has Declined* (2011), was born in Montréal, Canada, to Jewish parents in 1954. As a teenager he was, he says, "a true believer in Bakunin's anarchism."*[1] Mikhail Bakunin* was a Russian revolutionary and the founder of collectivist anarchism:* a political theory that argued for the abolition of the state, and for the tools and resources required for production to be collectively owned. But

Pinker's antipathy towards the state ended in October 1969, when he was 15, as a result of a police strike in Montréal. The police were protesting against the fact that their counterparts in Toronto, another Canadian city, were paid more than them. The events of the next day began Pinker's reflections about violence in society: "When law enforcement vanishes, all manner of violence breaks out ... By 11:20 a.m. the first bank was robbed ... This decisive empirical* test left my politics in tatters (and offered a foretaste of a life as a scientist)."[2] (An empirical test is a test founded on observable evidence rather than theory.)

Steven Pinker went on to study psychology* (the science of the human mind and its role in behavior) as an undergraduate at Dawson College, an institution in Montreal. He earned a masters degree in Canada at McGill University before completing a doctorate in experimental psychology at Harvard University in the United States. He now works at Harvard as the Johnstone Family Professor in the psychology department. Pinker's initial area of interest, however, was not the psychology of violence, but linguistics*—the study of language, in all its various aspects. His first book, *The Language Instinct*, was published in 1994. In it he defends the ideas of the American linguist Noam Chomsky,* who argues that all humans are "hardwired" with the same language-learning structural approach to language: in other words, we are not born as "blank states." In other books Pinker has explored human psychology and how our psychological functions have evolved. These interests are evident in *The Better Angels*.

## What Does *The Better Angels* Say?

In *The Better Angels* Steven Pinker states that human violence has declined over time. Though many assume that the world became more violent over the twentieth century, he argues the opposite. There is, he suggests, only an *impression* that violence is rising and that the future will bring even more violence. This impression is the result of our tendency to remember things that are easy to recall. We find it easier to remember shocking events that frighten us than events that seem more commonplace. In a feature written for the British *Guardian* newspaper in September 2015, Pinker says that this "is why we are more afraid of getting eaten by a shark than falling down the stairs, though the latter is likelier to kill us."[3] He argues that this tendency is exploited by a media that delights in showing violent events. As a result, we see the world as violent, rather than appreciating that it is *less* violent than it used to be. For Pinker, a number of important cultural changes that have occurred over the course of human history have shaped—and are still shaping—human psychology. These changes are making us less violent both as individuals and as a species.

Pinker uses statistical evidence to back his claim. His data includes figures for the deaths from wars, genocides,* and other large-scale violent events, as well as robberies and homicides across history.[4] He uses this to help identify the cultural and institutional forces that have caused the decline of violence. For Pinker these forces originate from the ideas of the "humanitarian Enlightenment,"* an intellectual movement that began in the eighteenth century, which placed a high value on human life. The Enlightenment helped to change society, and the social shifts it triggered also altered human psychology. The result, Pinker argues, was a decline in violence.

*The Better Angels* has several purposes. Pinker wants to counter the idea that violence is on the rise, noting that this common belief can have negative consequences: it prompts us to accept decisions based on fleeting impressions of danger, instead of decisions based on thought and reflection.[5] To correct this, Pinker provides an objective analysis of hard evidence and facts about the decline of violence. He also identifies the forces that have had an impact on this decrease, among which are the spread of democracy and the increasing tendency to see all human beings as citizens of a single community. In addition he points to changes in moral values and aesthetic tastes (that is, what might be considered "beautiful" or "ugly") that push us away from violence and toward pacifism.*

*The Better Angels* is descriptive. Pinker counters the idea that violence is rising by telling the story of how it has declined. He does so by identifying the trends of violence over history, and examines the reasons for the decrease by looking at historical changes. But *The Better Angels* also has a prescriptive* purpose: that is, Pinker discusses rules and tools that might be adopted to reduce violence further in the future.

## Why Does *The Better Angels* Matter?

Published in 2011, *The Better Angels* soon became a controversial work. It was immediately reviewed in all the major journals and newspapers, including the *New York Times*, the *New Yorker*, the *Guardian*, the *Economist*, the *Wall Street Journal*, *Nature*, and the *Financial Times*. Pinker is still reiterating the main claims of the book via the media; it remains a topic of discussion in the academic world, as well as in politics, economics, and society at large.

Pinker's work has helped to reshape debates about violence in the social sciences* (studies that encompass fields as diverse as anthropology, psychology, law, and economics). It has provided a starting point for fresh ways of thinking about the history of violence and the reasons for its decline. And it has revived interest in the study of statistical trends related to violence and the factors that trigger (or limit) it. As a result, the tools and conceptual analysis employed by Pinker in *The Better Angels* can be used in other areas of research to deepen our knowledge of violence.

More broadly, the work has been read and discussed by figures outside academia who are interested in social change. The American entrepreneur and philanthropist Bill Gates* wrote in his blog that *The Better Angels* "stands out as one of the most important books I've read—not just this year, but ever."[6] In 2015, Mark Zuckerberg,* the founder of the social networking service Facebook, started a book club on Facebook. *The Better Angels* was the second title chosen for the 2015 "Year of Books." Such endorsements illustrate the importance of *The Better Angels*, its relevance to public debates, and the impact it could have on the world.

The influence of the book is twofold: first, it helps raise awareness of the most pressing issues to do with violence; second, Pinker's analysis can be used to search for solutions to the problem of violence: it could help us create policies that foster and reinforce the social trends that may reduce violence further in the future.

## NOTES

1   Steven Pinker, *The Blank Slate: The Modern Denial of Human Nature* (London: Penguin Books, 2002), 331.

2   Steven Pinker, *The Better Angels of Our Nature: Why Violence Has Declined* (London: Penguin Books, 2011), 331.

3   Steven Pinker, "Now For The Good News: Things Really Are Getting Better," *Guardian*, September 11, 2015, accessed December 19, 2015, http://www.theguardian.com/commentisfree/2015/sep/11/news-isis-syria-headlines-violence-steven-pinker.

4   Pinker, *The Better Angels*, 1–30.

5   Pinker, *The Better Angels*, xxi.

6   Bill Gates, "My Bookshelf: *The Better Angels of Our Nature: Why Violence Has Declined*," June 18, 2012, accessed December 29, 2015, http://www.gatesnotes.com/Books/The-Better-Angels-of-Our-Nature.

# SECTION 1
# INFLUENCES

# THE AUTHOR AND THE HISTORICAL CONTEXT

## KEY POINTS

- *The Better Angels* contains a comprehensive review of statistical data about the trends of violence.

- It argues that violence has declined in recent centuries and presents a bold thesis about the causes of this decline.

- The second half of the twentieth century was characterized by a long period of peace. Steven Pinker grew up during this time and this may have shaped his ideas about the decline of violence.

### Why Read This Text?

Steven Pinker's *The Better Angels of Our Nature: Why Violence Has Declined* was published in 2011 and immediately sparked debate. The book discusses three key topics:

- The history of violence.
- The psychological* origins of violence.
- The institutional and cultural changes that can influence violence.

Pinker's thesis is that violence has declined over the course of history and that this decline will probably continue: "For all the violence that remains in the world, we are living in an extraordinary age ... [R] egardless of how the trends extrapolate into the future, something remarkable has brought us to the present."[1] He argues forcefully in

> ❝ This book grew out of an answer to the question, 'What are you optimistic about?' and I hope that the numbers I have marshaled have lifted your assessment of the state of the world from the lugubrious conventional wisdom. ❞
>
> Steven Pinker, *The Better Angels of Our Nature: Why Violence Has Declined*

favor of this positive outlook, using a large pool of data to support his arguments. And it is this combination of thought-provoking ideas, backed by his rigorous scientific methodology,* that makes the work important.

The impact of *The Better Angels* on the debate about violence is undeniable. All the major newspapers, including the *New Yorker*, the *New York Times*, the *Guardian*, and the *Financial Times*, have reviewed the book.[2] It has also started numerous academic and public discussions. Given its recent publication it is premature to predict its long-term influence on academic research, but its importance to current debate can be measured by the number of media references that have been made to it. As soon as a violent event hits the headlines, journalists contact Pinker for a reaction.[3] This happened after the rise of the Syrian conflict* in 2011, the start of the Ukrainian conflict* in 2013, and the 2015 attack on the satirical newspaper *Charlie Hebdo*.* In September 2015, Pinker published an opinion piece in the British newspaper the *Guardian* to claim that, despite these conflicts, violence is still in decline.[4]

## Author's Life

Steven Pinker was born in 1954 in Canada, the eldest of three children. His father was a lawyer and his mother a high-school vice-principal, while his brother now works as a policy analyst* in Canada (that is, he is engaged in determining the social consequences of public policy); both Steven Pinker and his sister are psychologists. The family is Jewish, but Pinker calls himself an atheist*[5] and criticizes the role that religion can play in supporting violence.

After studying psychology at Dawson College and at McGill University in Montréal, Pinker completed a doctorate in experimental psychology* (the study of the human mind and behavior in ways that can be measured) at Harvard University, under the supervision of the American psychologist Stephen Kosslyn.* He still lives in the United States, and is now Harvard's Johnstone Family Professor. Married three times, his current wife is the American novelist Rebecca Goldstein.* He acknowledges her influence on *The Better Angels*—in particular her role in bringing to his attention the importance of the Enlightenment.*[6] This was an intellectual movement with its roots in eighteenth-century Europe, characterized by the appeal to rationality and the defense of liberty, tolerance, and rights.

Prior to *The Better Angels,* Pinker was known for his work in the fields of psychology (the study of the human mind and behavior) and linguistics* (the study of the nature, history, and functioning of language); he published a number of academic texts and popular books. These helped to widen interest in the findings of cognitive science* (scientific inquiry into the operations, history, and faculties of the mind and brain), such as ideas about the origins of language and the functioning of our cognitive capacities. Pinker's scientific training provides the backbone for the statistical approach he uses in *The Better Angels.* This scientific methodology helps to support and strengthen the arguments in the book.

### Author's Background

Every day, we hear news of conflict, war, homicides, and robberies. The first half of the twentieth century witnessed two world wars* and several genocides.* So it has become common to think of the twentieth century as the most devastating period in human history: an era of truly global conflict in which war reached new heights of destructiveness. The early twenty-first century, meanwhile, has seen the rise of modern dangers such as climate change* and terrorism.* With the world around us torn apart by regional conflicts, religious extremism, and natural disasters, many analysts warn about the dangers of our times: warnings that are amplified by the media. The British journalist Roger Cohen* writes, "We are vulnerable and we are fearful."[7]

Pinker was born in the mid-twentieth century, the history of which had an influence on his ideas about violence. Instead of endorsing the mainstream opinion that humanity is becoming ever more destructive, however, he refutes this view; his statistical analysis shows that it is possible to reach a different conclusion. Pinker's training in scientific psychology and his secular education have helped shape his willingness to challenge opinions. His starting point was to try to look at human history objectively. Doing this spurred him to ask "why [there] has been so much violence in the past" and "why it has come down." These, he states, are "the two psychological questions that got me going."[8]

## NOTES

1   Steven Pinker, *The Better Angels of Our Nature: Why Violence Has Declined* (London: Penguin Books, 2011), 480.

2   Steven Pinker, "Review Excerpts for *The Better Angels of Our Nature*," accessed December 29, 2015, http://stevenpinker.com/content/review-excerpts-better-angels-our-nature.

3   Steven Pinker, "Has the Decline of Violence Reversed since The Better Angels of Our Nature was Written?" accessed December 29, 2015, http://stevenpinker.com/files/pinker/files/has_the_decline_of_violence_reversed_since_the_better_angels_of_our_nature_was_written.pdf?m=1410709356.

4   Steven Pinker, "Now For The Good News: Things Really Are Getting Better,"
     *Guardian*, September 11, 2015, accessed December 19, 2015, http://
     www.theguardian.com/commentisfree/2015/sep/11/news-isis-syria-
     headlines-violence-steven-pinker.

5   Steve Paulson, "Proud atheists," *Salon*, October 15, 2007, accessed
     December 29, 2015, http://www.salon.com/2007/10/15/pinker_goldstein/.

6   Steven Pinker, "Frequently Asked Questions about *The Better Angels of Our
     Nature: Why Violence Has Declined*," accessed December 29, 2015, http://
     stevenpinker.com/pages/frequently-asked-questions-about-better-angels-our-
     nature-why-violence-has-declined.

7   Roger Cohen, "A Climate of Fear," *New York Times*, October 27, 2014,
     accessed December 29, 2015, http://www.nytimes.com/2014/10/28/
     opinion/roger-cohen-a-climate-of-fear.html.

8   HSRP, "The Decline in Global Violence: Reality or Myth?" March 3, 2014,
     accessed December 29, 2015, http://www.hsrgroup.org/docs/Publications/
     HSR2013/HSR_2013_Press_Release.pdf.

# MODULE 2
## ACADEMIC CONTEXT

### KEY POINTS

- The study of violence is a complex multidisciplinary field. It interests researchers in anthropology* (the study of human beings via research into culture, society, and belief), history, sociology* (the study of the functioning of society and social behavior), economics,* political science* (the study of political institutions and political behavior), psychology* (the study of the human mind and behavior), and moral philosophy* (inquiry into the nature of "right behavior" and ethics).

- Researchers focus on different aspects of violence, and their interest depends on their field of study. Some explore its historical development, others its causes, and others its biological roots.

- *The Better Angels* brings together research from history, anthropology, and psychology.

### The Work in its Context

Steven Pinker's book *The Better Angels of Our Nature: Why Violence Has Declined* draws on work from a range of disciplines. It brings together the work of researchers who have looked at the trends of violence over time, and the relationships between violence, psychology, and human nature.

Pinker became interested in looking at the statistics for violence after reading the work of the American political scientist Ted Robert Gurr.*[1] In 1981, Gurr published a graph showing how homicide rates in England had declined by 95 percent between the thirteenth and twentieth centuries. Other academics had also gathered statistical

> ❝ [I]t was an interest in human nature and its moral and political implications, carried over from my earlier books ... Then in 2007, through a quirky chain of events, I was contacted by scholars in a number of fields who informed me there was far more evidence for a decline in violence than I had realized. Their data convinced me that the decline of violence deserved a book of its own. ❞
>
> Steven Pinker, "Frequently Asked Questions about *The Better Angels of Our Nature: Why Violence Has Declined*"

evidence about violence. Joshua Goldstein,[2] the eminent American scholar of international relations, had conducted research into the number of victims of wars, while the American political scientist Rudolph Rummel* had looked at the number of victims of genocides.*[3] Pinker used their data and methods in *The Better Angels*.

The study of violence raises several questions:

- How do we collect data about violence?
- How do we define violence?
- Can we infer any future trends about violence from the study of the past?
- Is violence an inherent aspect of human nature or is it the result of nurture (the environment, notably upbringing and parenting)?[4]

In other words, are humans born with certain characters and tendencies, or do they learn these as a result of their upbringing, society, and culture? Pinker starts his inquiry by examining this question, and later includes other issues.

21

His statistical approach also touches on issues concerning data: How is data collected? What do sets of data compare? What is the best way to collect data? Should data about other forms of aggression and conflict—domestic violence* or prison rates, for example—be studied? Political scientists and sociologists, as well as other academics, are currently debating which sources researchers should use.[5]

## Overview of the Field

The discussion about the interaction between nature and nurture* has a long history. The seventeenth-century English philosopher Thomas Hobbes* (1588–1679) thought that humans have an innate tendency to fight one another. Hobbes argued that only the presence of a strong state (the "Leviathan") can prevent permanent war.[6] In contrast, the eighteenth-century Geneva-born philosopher Jean-Jacques Rousseau* (1712–78) is credited with the development of the myth of the "noble savage."* This was the idea that when living in a state of nature* (in a band, or tribe, rather than in a state), humans are intrinsically good.[7]

These thinkers still influence contemporary anthropology, sociology, and psychology. Early anthropologists such as the Scottish diplomat John Crawfurd* were influenced by the notion of the "noble savage"; this continues to permeate some areas of current enquiry.[8] Other thinkers, such as the American scientist and historian Jared Diamond,* follow Hobbes and emphasize the brutality of the state of nature. These academics tend to characterize societies organized along non-state lines as living in a condition of perpetual conflict. The same divisions are seen in psychology. For those who subscribe to the empiricist* perspective, according to which knowledge comes from experience alone, humans are born as "blank slates"—all our psychological faculties, including violence, are acquired by means of "nurture." Countering this, the nativist* perspective argues that humans are born with some faculties, abilities, and bodies of knowledge.

In *The Better Angels* Pinker positions himself on the side of Hobbes, Diamond, and the nativists. But unlike Hobbes, Pinker does not think that human nature is intrinsically evil or inflexible; for him, it contains the psychological seeds both of violence and peaceable behavior. Nor does he consider the state to be the only entity that can reduce violence. For Pinker, this reduction can be traced to a change of attitude about the value of human life, which started with the cultural emphasis on reason and liberty produced by the intellectual and cultural current known as the Enlightenment* in the eighteenth century.

## Academic Influences

Pinker's inspiration came from a group of thinkers loosely connected by a shared core of ideas, rather than from a full-blown school of thought. He acknowledges, in particular, two very different figures as his primary influences: the English mathematician Lewis Fry Richardson* and the German-born sociologist* Norbert Elias.*

Lewis Richardson was an applied mathematician (roughly, a mathematician who conducts research for practical purposes), mostly known for his work on weather prediction. He was also one of the people who initiated the use of mathematical analysis in studying armed violence.[9] Pinker adopts Richardson's method of statistical analysis in exploring the history of violence.

From Norbert Elias, Pinker obtains his outlook on history. In his book *The Civilizing Process*, Elias puts forward the idea that since the end of the Middle Ages* there has been an increasing process of civilization in Europe, evidenced by changes of attitude toward violent behaviors, strengthening of social connectedness, and an increase in self-control. Elias identifies the forces that brought about this process of civilization and argues that it has resulted in a change in human psychology.[10]

Following in Elias's steps, Pinker tries to find the external causes that have transformed psychology and made humans less violent. He argues that ideas become integrated in social institutions and start to influence human psychology.[11] This blend of culture and cognitive psychology* (inquiry into mental processes such as thought, creativity, and memory) allows Pinker to bring nurture and nature back together.

## NOTES

1    Steven Pinker, *The Better Angels of Our Nature: Why Violence Has Declined* (London: Penguin Books, 2011), 60.

2    Joshua Goldstein, *Winning the War on War: The Surprising Decline in Armed Conflict Worldwide* (New York: Dutton, 2011).

3    Rudolph Rummel, *Death by Government* (New Brunswick, NJ: Transaction, 1994).

4    Nils Petter Gleditsch et al., "The Forum: The Decline of War," *International Studies Review* 15, no. 3 (2013): 396–419.

5    Gleditsch et al., "The Forum," 396–419.

6    Thomas Hobbes, *Leviathan* (Oxford: Clarendon Press, 2012).

7    Jean-Jacques Rousseau, *Discourse on the Origin of Inequality*, trans. Franklin Philip (Oxford: Oxford's World Classics, 2009).

8    Ted Ellingson, *The Myth of the Noble Savage* (Berkeley: University of California Press, 2001).

9    Lewis Fry Richardson, *Statistics of Deadly Quarrels* (Pittsburgh: Boxwood Press, 1960).

10   Norbert Elias, *The Civilizing Process*, trans. Edmund Jephcott (New York: Pantheon Books, 1982).

11   Pinker, *The Better Angels*, 694–6.

# MODULE 3
# THE PROBLEM

## KEY POINTS

- A central question for thinkers studying violence is: Can violence decrease over time, or is human nature too deeply connected to violent instincts to change?

- Steven Pinker takes the optimistic world view that violence has been declining, supporting his arguments with a statistical analysis of crimes, wars, and other violent events over the course of history.

- Pinker also proposes a theory about why and how violence has declined.

### Core Question

At the heart of Steven Pinker's book *The Better Angels of Our Nature: Why Violence Has Declined* is the question as to *why* it has declined. While the longest section of his work is devoted to the data that demonstrates the decrease, Pinker is not interested solely in trends, but in what causes them. He argues that while humans do have a psychological tendency to engage in conflict, they also possess the psychological ability to prevent violence. He goes on to explore the environmental and societal forces that have caused the decline, despite the existence of a certain inclination toward aggression.

Pinker was not the first thinker to look at the historical trends of violence. He says that his interest in this area was inspired by a book written by the Canadian evolutionary psychologists* Martin Daly* and Margo Wilson* (evolutionary psychology is the study of human and nonhuman psychology from the perspective of modern evolutionary theory). In *Homicide* (1988) Daly and Wilson suggest that

❝ But it is just as foolish to let our lurid imaginations determine our sense of the probabilities …The numbers tell us that war, genocide, and terrorism have declined over the past two decades—not to zero, but by a lot …The conditions that favored this happy outcome—democracy, prosperity, decent government, peacekeeping, open economies, and the decline of antihuman ideologies—are not, of course, guaranteed to last forever. But nor are they likely to vanish overnight. ❞

Steven Pinker, *The Better Angels of Our Nature: Why Violence Has Declined*

violent deaths have declined over the course of history. More recently this claim has been discussed and accepted more widely.[1]

Yet this idea can seem counterintuitive when looked at in the context of twentieth-century history—a period that witnessed two world wars,* genocides,* colonialism* (the exploitation and political domination of a land and people by a foreign power or people), and terrorism.* These events resulted in the commonly shared view that we are living in the most violent epoch of world history. Pinker's work directly challenges this belief. His originality lies in his argument that the decline of violence can be traced to changes in our values and our institutions. These, in turn, have influenced human psychology.

### The Participants

The problem of violence is at the heart of many political and societal debates, as well as being of interest to academics across many different fields. Historians tend to study the numerical data on violence; for example, the French historian Robert Muchembled* explores the trends of violence from the later Middle Ages* to the present day, and tries to find the roots of its decline. Like Pinker, he is interested in the ways in which male aggression has been tamed, and points to this as a reason.[2]

Anthropologists* have studied many aspects of violence, including its origins in human lineage and its development in various communities,[3] while evolutionary psychologists have attempted to find the biological and psychological roots of violence. Evolutionary psychologists also study the mechanisms (like morality) that aim to diminish conflict.[4] The American husband and wife team John Tooby* and Leda Cosmides* are pioneers in the field of evolutionary psychology. They have explored at length how our "natural instincts" and the modes of thought we learn from modern society interact and collide.

These are only a few examples of the participants in a vast field of study and public debate. But despite the many voices involved, the debate itself centers on very few oft-repeated claims and arguments.

### The Contemporary Debate

There are two broad debates in contemporary research. The first is about numbers: Is violence increasing or decreasing? The second is about the origins of violence: Where does violence come from—human biology, or society?

There is a view that attributes violence to society alone. Pinker aims to refute this. In 2000, 11 years before the publication of *The Better Angels*, he wrote a piece for the *New York Times* in which he stated, "The prevailing wisdom among many intellectuals has been that evil has nothing to do with human nature and must be attributed to political institutions."[5]

He goes on to challenge this, arguing that violence is part of human nature. But at the same time he tries to avoid the negative conclusions of this view by attempting to find a middle ground. He argues that if violence is part of human nature, it can be tamed by history and society. Pinker suggests that the rational ideas of the

Enlightenment* were key to this possibility. This view is similar to that of the British theoretical physicist David Deutsch.* In Pinker's words, Deutsch "defends the unfashionable view that the Enlightenment inaugurated an era of unlimited intellectual and moral progress."[6]

## NOTES

1   For example, John Mueller, "War Has Almost Ceased to Exist: An Assessment," *Political Science Quarterly* 124, no. 2 (2009): 297–321.

2   Robert Muchembled, *A History of Violence: From the End of the Middle Ages to the Present* (Cambridge: Polity Press, 2012).

3   Bettina Schmidt and Ingo Schröder, *Anthropology of Violence and Conflict* (New York: Psychology Press, 2001).

4   John Tooby and Leda Cosmides, "Groups in Mind: The Coalitional Roots of War and Morality," in *Human Morality and Sociality: Evolutionary and Comparative Perspectives*, ed. Henrik Hogh-Olesen (New York: Palgrave Macmillan, 2010), 91–234.

5   Steven Pinker, "All about Evil," *New York Times*, October 29, 2000, accessed December 22, 2015, http://www.nytimes.com/2000/10/29/books/all-about-evil.html.

6   Steven Pinker, "Stephen Pinker: By the Book," *New York Times: The Sunday Book Review*, September 25, 2014, accessed December 22, 2015, http://www.nytimes.com/2014/09/28/books/review/steven-pinker-by-the-book.html.

# MODULE 4
## THE AUTHOR'S CONTRIBUTION

### KEY POINTS

- Pinker has a balanced view of the origins of violence. He argues that some aspects of human psychology* tend toward violence, but that cultural and institutional forces can inhibit these tendencies.

- Pinker uses data from many sources to investigate levels of violence, both current and in the past.

- Pinker's moderate answer provides a proportionate view of the nature–nurture* debate: while violence is part of our human nature, external forces (nurture) can affect this.

### Author's Aims

In *The Better Angels of Our Nature: How Violence Has Declined*, Steven Pinker aims to challenge two assumptions about violence and human nature. The first is that violence has been steadily growing over the course of history.[1] The second is that we should be negative about the human condition. Pinker argues that while we are born with certain tendencies—an innate biological core of human psychology—this does not mean we are doomed to revert to violence. He challenges this "equation between a belief in a human nature and fatalism about the human condition."[2]

Pinker begins to build a complex but coherent picture of the interaction between psychology and the history of violence by presenting an overview of the data. He goes on to discuss the psychological factors that can encourage or inhibit violence. Finally he brings these discussions together and argues that over the centuries, human violence has declined, and that this decline is due to external

> **66** It's a natural topic for anyone interested in human nature. The question, 'Is our species innately violent and war-loving, or innately peaceful and cooperative?' goes back literally hundreds of years, maybe thousands. So it naturally falls under the category of psychology ... The worry is: if violence is in the genes—if we're killer apes and we have homicidal DNA—then there's nothing you can do about it. But this is a non sequitur. The answer is no, we don't have to be fatalistic. **99**
>
> Steven Pinker, interview in *Skeptical Inquirer*

forces that have tamed the human inclination toward violence—without eradicating it. This method allows him to redefine the question concerning the origins and decline of violence in terms of a complex interaction between internal (psychological) and external (institutional and cultural) factors.

Pinker partially achieves his aims in *The Better Angels*. The statistical trends he presents, though disputed, do show some decline in violence. And his claims about the interaction between history and psychology—while controversial—do have some coherence.

### Approach

Pinker takes an analytical approach in *The Better Angels*, starting from definitions, examining large collections of data, and then interpreting these in the light of his proposal. His definition of "violence" is any physical force used to cause damage or injury to others, excluding metaphorical violence, such as verbal aggression. He examines data in relation to two kinds of physical violence: that committed by private citizens (homicide, robbery, assault, and so on) and that committed by institutions (war, genocide,* capital punishment, and the like).

His data is gathered from various sources: forensic archeology (that is, archeology based on the analytical methods used at a crime scene) and ethnography* (the study of culture); town records; and the Uppsala Conflict Data Project and the Peace Research Institute in Oslo (resources hosted in Sweden and Norway respectively, which provide useful statistical and analytical information about violence and conflict resolution). In some cases, he uses data from historians and political scientists working on wars and genocides. Pinker always tries to be rigorous in his choice of data, stating his aim "was to use data only from sources that had a commitment to objectivity."[3] It is also important to note that he calculates the *relative* rate of violent crimes and not the absolute numbers. In other words, he calculates the number of victims of violence as a proportion of the population size. While there are more violent deaths now than in the past, this number has to be measured against the total size of the population. When the latter is taken into account, Pinker shows that there are far fewer violent deaths now than there were in the past.

Finally, Pinker uses ideas from philosophy,* sociology,* and psychology to uncover the bigger trends revealed by the data. Chief among these is the work of the German-born sociologist Norbert Elias.* Pinker uses Elias's book *The Civilizing Process* to explore the societal changes that have triggered the reduction of violence.

### Contribution in Context

*The Better Angels* is a highly original work in respect of its breadth, complexity, and interdisciplinary nature (the way it draws on the aims and methods of different academic disciplines). Pinker borrows the methodology of military historians and sociologists to gather data about violence. He then considers his findings using the methodology of evolutionary psychology* to examine how trends in the history of violence connect with human psychology.

The originality of the work stems from Pinker's ability to put together conceptual claims with empirical* data (that is, data verifiable by observation):

- While historians were gathering data that pointed to the decline of violence, they did not suggest any psychological interpretation of this trend.
- Psychologists were studying the biological roots of violence and the ways in which these factors could be changed.
- Some moral philosophers* were arguing that moral progress is being made, but without basing their claims on data.

In *The Better Angels* Pinker manages to bring all these lines of research together in a coherent argument.

While Pinker has been part of the field of cognitive science* (interdisciplinary inquiry into the mind and brain, often drawing on fields such as philosophy, neuroscience, and linguistics), he positions himself more as an independent thinker who does not belong in a strict sense to any school of thought. He nonetheless acknowledges his debt to many theorists, and says he is inspired by "humanitarian Enlightenment":* a secular and rational approach to inquiry, based on science.

## NOTES

1  Steven Pinker, *The Better Angels of Our Nature: Why Violence Has Declined* (London: Penguin Books, 2011), xxi–xxv.

2  Steven Pinker, "Frequently Asked Questions about *The Better Angels of Our Nature: Why Violence Has Declined*," accessed December 29, 2015, http://stevenpinker.com/pages/frequently-asked-questions-about-better-angels-our-nature-why-violence-has-declined.

3  Pinker, "Frequently Asked Questions."

# SECTION 2
## IDEAS

# MODULE 5
# MAIN IDEAS

## KEY POINTS

- Pinker sums up the psychological* roots of both human violence and peaceable nature by saying we possess "five demons and four Better Angels."

- He identifies our four "Better Angels" as empathy,* self-control, moral sense, and the faculty of reason.

- Pinker uses data and statistics because he wants to provide an objective analysis of the phenomenon of violence.

### Key Themes

In *The Better Angels of Our Nature: How Violence Has Declined*, Steven Pinker argues that violence has declined over the course of human history—a proposal contrasting with the popular impression that violence is increasing. As Pinker writes, "I have to convince you that violence really has gone down over the course of history, knowing that the very idea invites skepticism, incredulity, and sometimes anger."[1] To do so, he states, only hard evidence will help: "I will have to persuade you with numbers."[2]

The decrease in violence applies to both large-scale violence (conflict between states and nations), and small-scale violence (conflict within families and communities). Pinker offers a broad historical overview of the trend, spanning millennia. He begins his ambitious historical inquiry with prehistoric hunter-gatherers* (people who lived by hunting and collecting rather than developing agriculture) before turning to the Middle Ages* and arguing persuasively that medieval* society was permeated by violence. He continues to

> **❝** [V]iolence has declined over long stretches of time, and today we may be living in the most peaceable era in our species' existence … The historical trajectory of violence affects not only how life is lived but how it is understood. What could be more fundamental to our sense of meaning and purpose than a conception of whether the strivings of the human race over long stretches of time have left us better or worse off? **❞**
>
> Steven Pinker, *The Better Angels of Our Nature: How Violence Has Declined*

contemporary history and claims that despite two world wars,* the twentieth century saw a decline in violence.

Pinker then explores human psychology in an attempt to uncover the forces that have made us more peaceable. He identifies two opposing psychological forces: we are pushed toward violence by our "inner demons," and urged to cooperate and live in peace by the "The Better Angels of our nature" (an expression borrowed from the nineteenth-century American president Abraham Lincoln).* According to Pinker, psychology reveals that humans are neither intrinsically good nor intrinsically evil. On the contrary, "Human nature accommodates motives that impel us to violence … but also motives that … impel us toward peace."[3]

In the final part of the book, Pinker puts history and psychology together. He examines the external forces that have transformed (and are transforming) human psychology.

### Exploring the Ideas

Pinker outlines six historical transitions that have contributed to the decline of violence. The most important ones are:

- The "civilizing process"*—a term borrowed from the German-born sociologist* Norbert Elias* to denote a set of changes in institutions, values, and sensibilities that started in the Middle Ages, and helped to create more peaceful social attitudes.
- The "humanitarian revolution"—the appearance of a culture of pacifism,* tolerance, and secularism in eighteenth-century Europe, ushered in by the Enlightenment.*

Alongside these two fundamental historical forces Pinker identifies four other trends that have helped reduce violence:

- The absence of wars in Europe and the United States since World War II.*
- The decline in conflicts all over the world over the past 30 years.
- Stable economies.
- Stable democratic* political systems and the extension of human rights* to previously persecuted groups.

Pinker then looks at psychology. Here he identifies two opposing forces: the "five inner demons" that drive us toward violence and the "four Better Angels" that guide us toward peace and cooperation. He points out that from a psychological point of view, "aggression" is not a unified phenomenon but originates in five different psychological forces (the so-called demons). The "four Better Angels" are the psychological qualities that enable us to foster cooperation and altruism, or selfless behavior: empathy, self-control, moral sense, and the faculty of reason.

Looking at the interaction between history and psychology, Pinker identifies five external forces that have shaped human psychology and are driving the decline of violence:

- The presence of a strong state (in the governmental sense) that has an effective monopoly on violent action (through, for example, the police or military).
- The development of international commerce that requires peaceful exchange and stability.
- The increasing respect given to women and what are sometimes understood to be female values.
- The rise of modern means of transportation and communication.
- The increasing attention paid to rational, reasoned argument.

Together these forces encourage humans to listen to their "Better Angels" and silence their "inner demons."

### Language and Expression

*The Better Angels* is extremely well researched. Pinker's conclusions are based on extensive inquiry, facts, graphs, figures, and data. Despite this, the book is easy to read and the tone is accessible, conversational, or in Pinker's terms, "at times irreverent."[4] The book is intended for the general public, not only for specialists. Pinker's ambition is to reach a wide audience as well as to have an impact on current scholarship on violence and to foster academic debate and research.

Nevertheless, the work does use statistical tools, so a reader without any training in statistics might not fully understand how the data has been gathered and analyzed. But it is always explained and discussed, and the statistics used are fairly intuitive. In Pinker's words, "I will have to persuade you with numbers, which I will glean from datasets and depict in graphs. In each case I'll explain where the numbers came from and do my best to interpret the ways they fall into place."[5]

The colloquial language and the use of anecdotes, sometimes taken from Pinker's life (he characterizes the book, for example, as a "tale of six trends, five inner demons, four better angels, and five historical forces"[6]) make the overall argument easy to understand and follow.

## NOTES

1   Steven Pinker, *The Better Angels of Our Nature: Why Violence Has Declined* (London: Penguin Books, 2011), xxii.

2   Pinker, *The Better Angels*, xxii.

3   Pinker, *The Better Angels*, 483.

4   Pinker, *The Better Angels*, 696.

5   Pinker, *The Better Angels*, xxii.

6   Pinker, *The Better Angels*, xxiv.

# MODULE 6
# SECONDARY IDEAS

## KEY POINTS

- *The Better Angels* examines the relationship between religion, ideology,* and violence. (An ideology is a system of norms, beliefs, and theories held by a group or by individuals.)
- Pinker also evaluates the role of biology in prompting or reducing violence. He makes specific references to gender* differences—a theme largely overlooked in the debates that followed his work.
- Pinker's evaluation of the evolution of violence has had an impact on discussions in the field of evolutionary psychology.*

### Other Ideas

Steven Pinker's *The Better Angels of Our Nature: Why Violence Has Declined* is a complex work with a number of interconnected ideas; in it, Pinker also discusses many secondary ideas.

One of his key secondary ideas concerns the role of religion in the history of violence. While some thinkers claim that the Christian* religion has played a major role in fighting violence, Pinker opposes this view, instead looking at the Crusades* (the invasions of the Middle East by European Christian armies in the medieval* period) and the Inquisition* (an institution established by the Christian Church in the thirteenth century to ensure the purity of belief and religious practice, later notorious for the use of torture in the extraction of confessions) to underline its role in initiating conflicts and persecutions. His main claim in the book is that a secular* (nonreligious) process led to the development of secular liberal

> **❝** When it comes to the history of violence, the significant distinction is not one between theistic and atheistic regimes. It's the one between regimes that were based on demonizing, utopian ideologies (including Marxism, Nazism, and militant religions) and secular liberal democracies that are based on the ideal of human rights. **❞**
>
> Steve Pinker, "Frequently Asked Questions about *The Better Angels of Our Nature: Why Violence Has Declined"*

democracies* and to a reduction in violence.

Another important secondary issue is whether we have *evolved* as a species to be less violent. Pinker asks whether there has been a selection of traits that has favored peaceable individuals over violent ones, or whether human nature has remained unchanged over time. Although Pinker considers several pieces of evidence that could potentially support the idea that biological evolution* alters core human impulses, he ultimately rejects this idea. He explains that "while recent biological evolution may, in theory, have tweaked our inclinations toward violence and nonviolence, we have no good evidence that it actually has … At least for the time being [therefore], we have no need for that hypothesis."[1] His ultimate position is that human biology has remained unchanged over the timespan of the decline of violence (around 10,000 years).

### Exploring the Ideas

The thinkers who claim that religion has played a role in reducing violence often support their argument by stating that the major totalitarian* regimes of the twentieth century—the Nazism* of Germany in the years of World War II* and the various communist* regimes of Europe and Asia—were atheistic.*

Pinker responds to this by saying that it is not the fact that these regimes were atheistic that caused their violence, but the fact that they were all supported by a totalitarian ideology—their governments interceded in the lives of their citizens, aggressively suppressing dissent, as a point of political philosophy. In other words, they were driven by a doctrine that endorsed their violent behavior (for the Nazis, this was a belief in certain forms of racial superiority). Pinker argues that the doctrine-driven nature of the major totalitarian regimes gives them a fundamental similarity to religion. He goes on to contrast ideology-based regimes (both religious and nonreligious) with secular liberal democracies (the system of government dominant in the West today). He contends that it is within secular liberal democracies that violence declines.

While Pinker rejects the idea that nonviolent traits have evolved, he does consider how malleable human biology may be (that is, how easily it can be molded). The answer to this has consequences for the malleability of human psychology.* Pinker's position is that there is some degree of pliability, but that this mostly stems from how far the environment is able to favor the "Better Angels" over our "inner demons."

## Overlooked

One secondary idea that has been overlooked following the publication of *The Better Angels* is Pinker's discussion of the relationship between gender differences and violence. Males statistically show a greater propensity to violence than females. Pinker writes that "The rise and fall of testosterone* over the life span correlates, more or less, with the rise and fall of male pugnacity."*[2] (Pugnacity is the tendency to be aggressive.)

Pinker's view is that there are psychological (and biological) factors that make men more prone to violence. This does not mean that all men are violent, but it is to say that some biological factors make men more prone to aggression in some cultural and social contexts. Going on from this, Pinker argues that the "feminization" of society has been a factor in reducing violence. By feminization he means both the increase in the value accorded to "feminine qualities" (such as empathy)* and the political empowerment of women. This political empowerment includes developments such as an end to marriages in which the male partner holds all the power, the right of girls to be born, and women's control over reproduction.

The issue of gender difference is still a hot topic today. Pinker endorses "equity feminism":* the idea of legal equality between the sexes, according to which men and women should, for example, receive the same salary for doing the same work. But he argues that there are both biological and psychological differences between the genders;[3] in his book *The Blank Slate* (2002), he writes that "women and men do not have interchangeable minds … people have desires other than power…"[4]

In *The Better Angels*, Pinker discusses gender differences and their role in the history of violence. As well as offering insights into possible measures for reducing violence, his ideas could have an important impact in areas such as education.

## NOTES

1   Steven Pinker, *The Better Angels of Our Nature: Why Violence Has Declined* (London: Penguin Books, 2011), 620–1.

2   Pinker, *The Better Angels*, 519.

3   Steven Pinker and Elizabeth Spelke, "The Science of Gender and Science. Pinker vs. Spelke," *Edge: The Third Culture*, May 16, 2005, accessed December 22, 2015, Edge.org/3rd_culture/debate05/debate05_index.html.

4   Steven Pinker, *The Blank Slate: The Modern Denial of Human Nature* (London: Penguin Books, 2002), 343.

# MODULE 7
# ACHIEVEMENT

## KEY POINTS

- *The Better Angels* challenges a pessimistic view of history by providing robust statistical data about the decline of violence over the course of human history.

- It also aims to discover the cultural and psychological* causes behind the decline in violence. Pinker's achievements in this regard are disputed.

- One issue with Pinker's data is that it is mostly limited to the Western world.

### Assessing the Argument

In writing *The Better Angels of Our Nature: Why Violence Has Declined*, Steven Pinker had two clear aims. He wanted to show that violence has been steadily declining over time, despite our impressions to the contrary. And he wanted to discover the reasons behind that decline.

Pinker's first aim is achieved through an impressive marshaling of data. The book contains around 100 graphs[1] gathered from a variety of sources. These show a downward trend in violence, both on a small scale (in families and communities) and a large scale (among nations and states). Pinker is also successful in explaining why—despite the data—we have the impression that violence is growing: "If you base your beliefs about the state of the world on what you read in the news, your beliefs will be incorrect. [It's] about things that happen, particularly bad things—and [given] ]the nature of human cognition [people] base their estimates of risk on how easily they can recall examples from memory."[2]

Pinker's second aim was to discover *why* violence has declined. He

> ❝ *The Better Angels of Our Nature* is a supremely important book. To have command of so much research, spread across so many different fields, is a masterly achievement. Pinker convincingly demonstrates that there has been a dramatic decline in violence, and he is persuasive about the causes of that decline. ❞
>
> Peter Singer, *Is Violence History?*

attributes this to the emergence of cultural and institutional forces such as democracy,* the growth of economic exchanges and of cosmopolitanism*—the belief that all human beings are citizens of a single community—which leads to an increase in cultural and information exchange. These forces have led to institutional changes that support more peaceful societies.

In this regard, Pinker's thesis remains possible, but not proven. Violence is a complex and multifaceted phenomenon. As a result, we lack robust scientific evidence that shows the impact of institutional changes on the decline of violence. This is not to say that Pinker's thesis is false. His thesis shows that the decline in violence *correlates* (perhaps robustly) with some cultural changes. But he is not able to establish unequivocally that these changes were responsible for the decline of violence.

## Achievement in Context

*The Better Angels* has been an undeniable commercial success: a bestseller that sparked a vigorous debate. Its success was probably boosted by its timely publication in 2011. This coincided with the popular uprisings in the Middle East and North Africa that began in 2010 known as the Arab Spring* and the death of the terrorist leader Osama bin Laden:* two events that seemed—at the time—to support

Pinker's claims.

Pinker's thesis that violence is in decline is based on empirical*
data: observed, factual information. As with all truly empirical claims,
it is open to falsification (being proven wrong). This means that the
validity and achievement of this work depends on data continuing to
support it.

In relation to this, Pinker recently examined new data that had
been gathered between 2011 and 2015. He concluded that "[the]
global trends since the completion of *The Better Angels of Our Nature*
show no reversal of the historical decline of violence, and in every case
except the effects of the conflict in Syria,* a continuation of the
decline."[3]

Despite its limitations, *The Better Angels* is an achievement. Maybe
the most balanced assessment of its success comes from the British
political scientist Adam Roberts,* who wrote that "with all its
imperfections, [the book] is much the most interesting work available
on the terrifying subject of violence in history. It may be meta-history,
but it is wonderfully illuminating."

### Limitations
*The Better Angels* does have some shortcomings, however. These are
evident both in the data Pinker has analyzed and in the conceptual
framework he employs.

The data poses three key problems:

- Pinker compares data on violent deaths in timeframes that
  are distant from each other, such as the eighteenth and the
  twentieth century. This is problematic because we have only
  limited records of events in the past, and because comparing
  two very distant and different periods is necessarily based on
  an oversimplification of conditions and circumstances.

- Pinker does not always take into account deaths that are *indirectly* caused by wars. The Australian academic Jeff Lewis* challenges this exclusion of data on after-war mortality. He notes that wars always trigger follow-on civilian deaths, due to the lowering of living standards, sickness, and suicides. The inclusion of such data would increase the war mortality rate.
- Pinker's dataset is geographically limited, mostly to the United States and Europe; the rest of the world is largely overlooked. The American journalist Elizabeth Kolbert* writes, "The scope of Pinker's attentions is almost entirely confined to Western Europe."[4] She criticizes the absence of a discussion of the violence inherent in colonialism* (the exploitation of one territory and people by a dominant foreign power or people) and its impact on the colonized countries.

Another limitation of the book is Pinker's definition of violence, which is any use of physical force used to cause damage or injury in others. He does not include verbal, metaphorical, or economic violence. Even more importantly, he does not include the deeds of democratic states that could be regarded as state violence, such as increasing imprisonment rates in the United States and the mistreatment of prison inmates. This limited definition may have an impact on the scope of Pinker's claims.

## NOTES

1   Steven Pinker, "Graphic Evidence: Steven Pinker's Optimism on Trial," *Guardian*, September 11, 2015, accessed December 22, 2015, http://www.theguardian.com/commentisfree/ng-interactive/2015/sep/11/graphic-evidence-steven-pinkers-optimism-on-trial.

2   Steven Pinker, "Has the Decline of Violence Reversed since *The Better Angels of Our Nature* was Written?" accessed December 22, 2015,

http://stevenpinker.com/files/pinker/files/has_the_decline_of_violence_
reversed_since_the_better_angels_of_our_nature_was_written.
pdf?m=1410709356.

3    Pinker, "Has the Decline of Violence Reversed?"

4    Elizabeth Kolbert, "Peace in Our Time: Steven Pinker's History of Violence,"
     *New Yorker*, October 3, 2011, accessed December 22, 2015, http://www.
     newyorker.com/magazine/2011/10/03/peace-in-our-time-elizabeth-kolbert.

# MODULE 8
# PLACE IN THE AUTHOR'S WORK

## KEY POINTS

- Pinker's body of work has focused on human psychology,* its functioning, and its evolutionary origins.

- *The Better Angels* is Pinker's 13th book and one of his most controversial best sellers.

- *The Better Angels* connects Pinker's work on the functioning of human psychology with a broader exploration of history and culture.

### Positioning

When *The Better Angels of Our Nature: Why Violence Has Declined* was published in 2011, Steven Pinker was already known as one of the most influential authors of popular books on cognitive science.* *The Better Angels* is more ambitious than his previous works: Pinker steps outside of his area of expertise (cognitive science)* to integrate psychology with history, sociology,* and economics.* Pinker has explained in several interviews that he has been thinking about the issues discussed in *The Better Angels* since at least 2007. Its subject matter connects with his exploration of human nature in two of his earlier books, *The Blank Slate: The Modern Denial of Human Nature* (2002) and *The Stuff of Thought: Language as a Window into Human Nature* (2007).[1]

While Pinker has frequently discussed the issues of the book over the past four years, he has not written a major publication on the topic of violence since *The Better Angels*. His most recent work is *The Sense of Style: The Thinking Person's Guide to Writing in the 21st Century* (2014). As the title suggests, it aims to help people achieve a clear and accessible

> 66 Human nature is a complex system with many
> components. It comprises mental faculties that lead us
> to violence, but also faculties that pull us away from
> violence, such as empathy, self-control, and a sense
> of fairness. It also comes equipped with open-ended
> combinatorial faculties for language and reasoning,
> which allow us to reflect on our condition and
> figure out better ways to live our lives. This vision of
> psychology, together with a commitment to secular
> humanism, has been a constant in my books, though it
> has become clearer to me in recent years. 99
>
> Steve Pinker, "Frequently Asked Questions about *The Better Angels of Our Nature: Why Violence Has Declined"*

writing style. This is a departure from previous subjects he has explored, but like his earlier books, *The Sense of Style* is profoundly informed by up-to-date research in psychology and science.

### Integration

The main focus of Pinker's career has been human psychology and its place in nature and society. *The Better Angels* expands this, integrating the question of human psychology into a broader historical context. In this respect it is one of his most ambitious works.

Pinker's early works looked at experimental psychology\* (the study of the human mind and behavior using scientific methodology) and linguistics\* (the study of the various things that together serve to define language). He worked with the American cognitive scientist Stephen Kosslyn\* on mental imagery (the way we represent the world to ourselves) and the representation of three-dimensional space. Later he looked at how infants acquire irregular verbs when learning language. His research on this was popularized in his *Words and Rules:*

*The Ingredients of Language* (1999).[2]

By then, Pinker had already produced two best sellers. His first was *The Language Instinct* (1994), which introduced the American linguist Noam Chomsky's* work on language to a popular audience. Chomsky argues that the rules of language are innate: learning only triggers something that was already present and stored in the mind. Pinker defends this view against the opposing idea: that we are born as a clean slate and that language is a social construct imposed from outside.

In 1997 he produced another best seller, *How the Mind Works*. This, along with *The Blank Slate: The Modern Denial of Human Nature* (2002) and *The Stuff of Thought: Language as a Window into Human Nature* (2007) focuses on psychology more generally. These books introduce the ideas of contemporary experimental cognitive science and evolutionary psychology* to the public.

*The Blank Slate* anticipates some of the ideas discussed in *The Better Angels*. In this book Pinker refutes the idea that the mind is an empty canvas ready to be filled in by culture and society. He argues that it is shaped by evolution,* and fixed. Society has only a limited ability to change it: "The denial of human nature has spread beyond the academy and has led to a disconnect between intellectual life and common sense."[3] In *The Better Angels*, he again explores the relationship between evolution and psychology.

## Significance

*The Better Angels* helped to establish Pinker as one of the most influential thinkers of our time. Given the variety of topics and fields he has worked in, it is not easy to establish whether this title is his best or most important work. It is difficult, for instance, to compare it to his academic research on mental imagery or on children's acquisition of irregular verbs. But what is certain is that while Pinker's scientific work and popular books about psychology made him an acclaimed cognitive scientist, *The Better Angels* established him as a global thinker. Indeed, in 2013 he was named the third most influential thinker of the year by *Prospect* magazine. As the British journalist John Dugdale writes, "Pinker might well have made the chart anyway, but probably owes his high position to his switch from his specialist field of psycholinguistics to history in *The Better Angels of Our Nature.*"[4] In 2014 he was rated number 26 among the top 100 thinkers by the American bimonthly magazine *Foreign Policy*.[5]

As these references show, *The Better Angels* helped establish Pinker's fame beyond his original field of expertise. He is now at the center of debates on the most pressing contemporary issues.

## NOTES

1   Steven Pinker, "Frequently Asked questions About *The Better Angels of Our Nature: Why Violence Has Declined*," accessed December 22, 2015, http://stevenpinker.com/pages/frequently-asked-questions-about-better-angels-our-nature-why-violence-has-declined, accessed September 15, 2015.

2   Steven Pinker, *Words and Rules: The Ingredients of Language* (New York: HarperCollins, 1999).

3   Steven Pinker, *The Blank Slate: The Modern Denial Of Human Nature* (London: Penguin, 2002), 14.

4   John Dugdale, "Richard Dawkins Named World's Top Thinker in Poll," *Guardian*, April 23, 2013, accessed December 22, 2015, http://www.theguardian.com/books/booksblog/2013/apr/25/richard-dawkins-named-top-thinker.

5   *Foreign Policy*, "A World Disrupted: The Leading Global Thinkers of 2014," accessed December 30, 2015, http://globalthinkers.foreignpolicy.com.

# SECTION 3
## IMPACT

# MODULE 9
# THE FIRST RESPONSES

## KEY POINTS

- The reaction to *The Better Angels* was polarized. The negative reviews disputed either Pinker's conceptual assumptions or his use and interpretation of the data.

- Pinker has replied to some of these criticisms in journal articles and interviews, either by presenting more data or by restating his conceptual points.

- Many of his critics remain unconvinced by his replies: their reactions allow for a more balanced view of the book.

### Criticism

Steven Pinker's *The Better Angels of Our Nature: Why Violence has Declined* received mixed reviews.[1] The Australian moral philosopher* Peter Singer* called it a "supremely important book,"[2] while the American political scientist Robert Jervis* finds that the trends discovered by Pinker "are not subtle—many of the changes involve an order of magnitude or more. Even when his explanations do not fully convince, they are serious and well-grounded."[3]

While many academics agree that Pinker's numbers show a downward trend in violence, critics tend to disagree with the explanations for it.[4] For example, the American academic Bradley A. Thayer* thinks that the decline is more plausibly due to power balances in the West, and argues that it is more fragile than Pinker thinks.[5] Others say that Pinker does not give enough weight to material and institutional factors, as opposed to cultural ones.[6]

Pinker's critics can be divided into two groups: the first questions the book's conceptual foundations; the second underlines the

> ❝ Steven Pinker's *The Better Angels of Our Nature:Why Violence Has Declined* stands out as one of the most important books I've read—not just this year, but ever ...The book is about violence, but paints a remarkable picture that shows the world has evolved over time to be a far less violent place than before. It offers a really fresh perspective on how to achieve positive outcomes in the world. ❞
>
> Bill Gates, *My Bookshelf*

shortcomings of its data.

The dispute with this second group is methodological: where and how can data on mortality be gathered, and how should it be interpreted? The Lebanese American statistician Nassim Nicholas Taleb[*] points to some fallacies in Pinker's statistical analysis,[7] stating that his "estimation from past data has monstrous errors. A record of the people who died in the last few years has very very little predictive powers of how many will die the next year, and is biased downward. One biological event can decimate the population."[8] The Australian academic Jeff Lewis,[*] meanwhile, accuses Pinker of relying on a very small dataset and points out that the exclusion of after-war mortality data is problematic.

## Responses

The critics who question Pinker's conceptual approach in *The Better Angels* include the British political philosopher John Gray[*] and the American journalist Elizabeth Kolbert.[*] Gray says that Pinker is wrong in thinking that science and humanism[*] belong together. Referencing the broad legacy of the nineteenth-century naturalist Charles Darwin,[*] a pioneering figure in the history of evolutionary science[*] and the rational social philosophy of humanism,[*] Gray writes, "Science and humanism are at odds more often than they are at one. For a devoted Darwinist like Pinker to maintain that the world is being pacified by the spread of a particular world view is deeply ironic. There is nothing in Darwinism to suggest that ideas and beliefs can transform human life."[9]

In the same vein, Elizabeth Kolbert observes that the very forces that produced Pinker's moral progress were also responsible for some of history's worst atrocities; referencing two twentieth-century totalitarian* systems, she writes, "Though Pinker would like to pretend otherwise, Fascism and Communism are ... every bit as modern as women's rights and the Eurozone."*[10]

In response, Pinker restates his position:[11] he does not claim that the world feels less dangerous, but he claims that it is—objectively—less violent.[12] He claims that Taleb seems to misunderstand the whole project of *The Better Angels*: that it is descriptive, not predictive,[13] and that he is not trying to present a prediction about violence in the future.[14] The problem outlined by Taleb is not, therefore, relevant to the book's interpretation of why violence *has* declined.

Against critics such as Lewis, Pinker remarks that they focus only on specific examples in his data, and do not look at the whole picture. Even if some of the data is indeed imprecise, the global picture still shows a decline in violence.

These discussions have not resulted in major revisions to the work. They have, however, forced Pinker to return to his claims and support them with more data.

## Conflict and Consensus

Despite the popularity of *The Better Angels*, there is very little agreement about the major claims of the book, and many of its critics remain unconvinced. But Pinker's data on the trends of violence have been the subject of a consensus. Indeed, a 2012 document from the Human Security Report Project* discusses Pinker's book and concludes, "Today there is broad agreement within the research community that the number and deadliness of interstate wars has declined dramatically."[15]

Pinker was not the first to show that there has been a decline in violence over the centuries. As a result, it is not clear whether this consensus about it was reached thanks to him, or if was already present in some fields, such as history and criminology* (a field of research concerned with the exploration, understanding, and prevention of criminal behavior in individuals and societies). Either way, Pinker presents original data that had not been compiled before. From this point of view he contributed original research to the debate.

Following the attack by terrorists on the French satirical magazine *Charlie Hebdo** in Paris and the ongoing conflict in Syria,* Pinker has returned to his proposal. Referencing the long period of global tension known as the Cold War,* which ended in 1991 with the final collapse of the communist Soviet Union,* Pinker published an article in September 2015 in the British *Guardian* newspaper in which he argued, "I put my optimism on trial by updating my graphs ... Discouragingly, the precipitous decline in the number of civil wars after the end of the cold war, from 26 in 1992 to four in 2007, has bent back up to 11 in 2014 ... One of these wars, in Syria, also caused a small bounce in the global rate of war deaths after a vertiginous six-decade plunge ... The good news is that this is the only bad news: the rate of every other kind of violence has stuck to its recent low or declined even further."[16]

## NOTES

1   A list of reviews can be found at Cognitive Science Perspectives on Conflict, Violence, Peace and Justice (course outline), accessed December 30, 2015, http://web.stanford.edu/class/symsys203/.

2   Peter Singer, "Is Violence History?" *New York Times*, October 6, 2011, accessed December 30, 2015, http://www.nytimes.com/2011/10/09/

books/review/the-better-angels-of-our-nature-by-steven-pinker-book-review.
html.

3   Robert Jervis, "Pinker the Prophet," *National Interest*, Nov–Dec 2011,
    accessed December 30, 2015, http://nationalinterest.org/bookreview/
    pinker-the-prophet-6072.

4   Nils Petter Gleditsch et al., "The Forum: The Decline of War," *International
    Studies Review* 15, no. 3 (2013): 396–419.

5   Bradley A. Thayer, "Humans, not Angels: Reasons to Doubt the Decline
    of War Thesis," in "The Forum: The Decline of War," *International Studies
    Review* 15, no. 3 (2013): 407.

6   Jack S. Levy and William R. Thompson, "The Decline of War: Multiple
    Trajectories and Diverging Trends," in "The Forum: The Decline of War,"
    *International Studies Review* 15, no. 3 (2013): 412.

7   Nassim Nicholas Taleb, "The 'Long Peace' is a Statistical Illusion,"
    accessed December 30, 2015, http://www.fooledbyrandomness.com/
    longpeace.pdf.

8   Nassim Nicholas Taleb, Facebook, accessed December 30, 2015, https://
    www.facebook.com/permalink.php?story_fbid=10151641931853375&
    id=13012333374.

9   John Gray, "Delusions of Peace," *Prospect*, September 21, 2011, accessed
    December 30, 2015, http://www.prospectmagazine.co.uk/features/john-
    gray-steven-pinker-violence-review.

10  Elizabeth Kolbert, "Peace in Our Time: Steven Pinker's History of Violence,"
    *New Yorker*, October 3, 2011, accessed December 22, 2015, http://www.
    newyorker.com/magazine/2011/10/03/peace-in-our-time-elizabeth-kolbert.

11  For the debate, see John Gray, "John Gray: Steven Pinker is wrong about
    violence and war," *Guardian*, March 13, 2015, accessed December 30,
    2015, http://www.theguardian.com/books/2015/mar/13/john-gray-steven-
    pinker-wrong-violence-war-declining.

12  Steven Pinker, "Frequently Asked Questions about *The Better Angels of Our
    Nature: Why Violence Has Declined*," accessed December 30, 2015, http://
    stevenpinker.com/pages/frequently-asked-questions-about-better-angels-our-
    nature-why-violence-has-declined.

13  Steven Pinker, "Fooled by Belligerence. Comments on Nassim Taleb's 'The
    Long Peace is a Statistical Illusion,'" accessed December 30, 2015, http://
    stevenpinker.com/files/comments_on_taleb_by_s_pinker.pdf.

14  Pinker, "Fooled by Belligerence."

15  HSRP, "The Decline in Global Violence: Reality or Myth?" March 3, 2014,

accessed December 29, 2015, http:/www.hsrgroup.org/docs/Publications/ HSR2013/HSR_2013_Press_Release.pdf.

16 Steven Pinker, "Now For The Good News: Things Really Are Getting Better," *Guardian*, September 11, 2015, accessed December 19, 2015, http:/www. theguardian.com/commentisfree/2015/sep/11/news-isis-syria-headlines-violence-steven-pinker.

# MODULE 10
# THE EVOLVING DEBATE

## KEY POINTS

- *The Better Angels* offers (to date) the most comprehensive data in support of the claim that violence is declining.

- While we cannot talk about a "school of thought" emerging from *The Better Angels*, a broad group of thinkers and public figures have been inspired by the text.

- The book has influenced not only members of the academic world, but also entrepreneurs such as the American cofounder of Microsoft, Bill Gates,* and the American cofounder of Facebook, Mark Zuckerberg.*

### Uses and Problems

Steven Pinker's *The Better Angels of Our Nature: Why Violence Has Declined* was published in 2011. It is therefore too early to chart its influence on other authors. Nonetheless, we can gauge how this influence may develop in the uses made of the text in the years since its publication. Several studies on trends of violence cite the text.[1] The 2014 special volume of the peer-reviewed journal *Evolutionary Psychology* focuses on the evolution of violence and makes many references to *The Better Angels*.[2] Across a wide range of disciplines in the social sciences, readers have responded to *The Better Angels* by modifying, completing, and criticizing some of its shortcomings.

For example, in a publication of 2015, historians and sociologists working on the history of crime assessed the decline of homicide in 55 countries since 1950. They found that the downward trend in violence has been widespread.[3] They refer to Pinker's work in the paper, but contrary to the proposal of *The Better Angels* they did not find a strong

> ❝ In April 2012, we invited dozens of scholars from around the USA to join us at Oakland University in Rochester, Michigan for a day-long interdisciplinary conference on 'The Evolution of Violence.' This conference followed a visit and lecture the day before by Steven Pinker on his recent book, *The Better Angels of Our Nature.* We invited as panelists some of the leading violence scholars from many different disciplines, including psychology, criminology, biology, anthropology, archeology, law, philosophy, and medicine. ❞
>
> Todd K. Shackelford and Ranald D. Hansen, *Preface to The Evolution of Violence*

connection between the decline of violence and modernization* (the process of the transformation of societies from preindustrial, traditional, agrarian, and religious to fully industrial, urban, and secular). While all 55 countries showed signs of declining violence, only rich and Western-style democracies* showed this connection. They concluded with a more modest take on Pinker's thesis: "The view that violent crimes are on the decline because modernization is transforming the world ... is an exceedingly broad one. Our study is limited to a single type of violence, over a 60-year time frame, and based on an examination of a non-random sample of mostly wealthy western-style democracies. For this highly select undertaking, high modernization does not provide a complete explanation and yet such a view fits the data better than a conflict view."[4]

## Schools of Thought

There are two principle reasons why *The Better Angels* has yet to create a school of thought. One is that it was published very recently and it is too early to assess its long-term influence. The other is that the scope of the book is broad and encompasses many disciplines. As a result, it might be having an influence without creating a cohesive set of thinkers who identify explicitly with the ideas presented in the book.

*The Better Angels* has a place within a general world view that can be broadly defined as optimistic about the progress of humanity. According to Pinker, thinkers and philosophers who have taken this view include the French philosopher Auguste Comte,* the English philosophers John Stuart Mill,* Thomas Hobbes,* and John Locke,* the Scottish economist* David Hume,* and the German philosopher* Immanuel Kant.* And the book appeals to many thinkers from different areas, both inside and outside academia. The American technologists and philanthropists Bill Gates and Mark Zuckerberg both admire the text, as do prominent academics including the Australian philosopher Peter Singer* and the British political scientist* Adam Roberts.*[5] Singer declared it a "supremely important book."[6] The book, for them, gives hope for real progress (maybe a moral progress in Singer's case) in history.

## In Current Scholarship

So far no clear disciple or successor has emerged who shares *The Better Angels'* overall project. There are, however, many researchers who use the work as a starting point for their scientific inquiries. In the field of anthropology,* several researchers are investigating the biological and cultural origins of violence. They are using Pinker's book either to develop his proposals in more detail, or as a negative starting point. For example, some have accepted his claim that violence declines as people move from hunter–gatherer* societies to societies organized along the lines of a state.[7] Others oppose this view; for them, hunter–gatherer societies are not considerably more violent than state societies.*[8] Like Pinker, they base their claims on data and on available evidence.

Another example of the use of *The Better Angels* in current scholarship is in evolutionary psychology.* Here the book forms the starting point for a debate about the biological origins of violence; the editors of a special volume on the evolution of violence acknowledge their debt to the work.[9] A final example is in international politics, which has also referenced *The Better Angels* in discussions. In 2013, the peer-reviewed journal *International Studies Review* carried a piece stating that "several authors have announced a 'waning of war' in recent decades (including a cognitive psychologist with a massive 800-page tome (Pinker 2011))." It continues, "Despite the breadth of this literature, this is not the end of the argument, but rather the start of a long debate."[10]

## NOTES

1   Timothy Kohler et al., "The Better Angels of Their Nature: Declining Violence Through Time Among Prehispanic Farmers of the Pueblo Southwest," *American Antiquity* 79, no. 3 (2014): 444–64.

2   Todd Kennedy Shackelford and Ranald D. Hansen, *The Evolution of Violence* (New York: Springer Verlag, 2014).

3   Gary LaFree et al., "How Effective Are Our 'Better Angels'? Assessing Country-level Declines in Homicide Since 1950," *European Journal of Criminology* 12, no. 4 (2015): 482–504.

4   LaFree et al., "How Effective Are Our 'Better Angels'?," 495.

5   Adam Roberts, "The Long Peace Getting Longer," *Survival* 54, no. 1 (2012): 175–83.

6   Peter Singer, "Is Violence History?" *New York Times*, October 6, 2011, accessed December 30, 2015, http://www.nytimes.com/2011/10/09/books/review/the-better-angels-of-our-nature-by-steven-pinker-book-review.html.

7   Nam C. Kim, "Angels, Illusions, Hydras, and Chimeras: Violence and Humanity," *Reviews in Anthropology* 41, no. 4 (2012): 239–72.

8   Geoffrey Benjamin et al., "Violence: Finding Peace," *Science* 338, no. 6105 (2012): 327.

9   Shackelford and Hansen, *The Evolution of Violence*.

10  Nils Petter Gleditsch et al., "The Forum: The Decline of War," *International Studies Review* 15, no. 3 (2013): 396–419.

# MODULE 11
# IMPACT AND INFLUENCE TODAY

## KEY POINTS

- *The Better Angels* is still at the center of debates on the history and origins of violence.
- Pinker's book continues to challenge the received view that the present is the most violent era in human history.
- Critics of the book take a broadly negative world view of humanity and its future.

### Position

Steven Pinker's book *The Better Angels of Our Nature: Why Violence Has Declined* defends the optimistic idea that violence has been steadily declining over the course of history. The book's central claims are still discussed and cited. His ideas have been referenced in recent work on morality and empathy,[*][1] and used to explore the trends of violence in new geographical areas and at different moments in history.[2] The text is also referenced in current debates about violence.[3]

One area in which the book contributes to ongoing debates concerns the relation between violence and climate change.[*] Pinker mentions global warming,[*] but he suggests that it will not have a significant impact on levels of violence. His argument is that conflicts are more likely to occur in poor and politically unstable countries than in countries that suffer natural disasters, "since the state of the environment is at most one ingredient in a mixture that depends far more on political and social organization, [wars over resources] are far from inevitable, even in a climate-changed world."[4] Pinker reasons that strongly democratic[*] and wealthy countries can react promptly to natural disasters and contain their consequences. This helps them avoid

> 66 *The Better Angels of Our Nature* is a supremely important book ... But what of the future? Our improved understanding of violence, of which Pinker's book is an example, can be a valuable tool to maintain peace and reduce crime, but other factors are in play. 99
>
> Peter Singer, *Is Violence History?*

the possibly violent ramifications of these events.

The book has revived interest in the study of statistical trends related to violence and in the study of factors that trigger (or limit) violence. The current consensus is that *The Better Angels* is a key reference book for any discussion of these issues. It is, though, too early to say whether this trend will continue.

### Interaction

Drawing on the aims and methods of different academic fields, *The Better Angels* is an interdisciplinary work. Pinker's inspiration came partly from his desire to challenge the idea, widespread in the social sciences,* that humans are blank slates. To those who subscribe to this belief, there are no innate biological or psychological* faculties: everything comes from society and culture (an idea Pinker attributes to the followers of the influential German American anthropologist* Franz Boas).*[5] If this is true, violence cannot be a biological phenomenon; it is merely societal and cultural. Pinker challenges this view and argues that people have some innate predispositions toward violence. He also suggests that these may, to some degree, be tamed through historical processes.

*The Better Angels* also challenges the view that violence is rising. These challenges have sparked an immediate response: for example, the British philosopher* John Gray* reacted to Pinker's underlying conceptions of human nature and history. Gray expresses a negative, pessimistic view of human nature and adopts a broadly Hobbesian* world view; the seventeenth-century English philosopher Thomas Hobbes argued that humans are selfish and self-serving, and that without a powerful government to hold these impulses in check, we live in a state of perpetual conflict. Gray's opinions of humanity and its future are radically different to those of Pinker. It is unsurprising, then, that there are differences between them on the subject of human violence.

## The Continuing Debate

The debate between Pinker and his opponents is less about Pinker's text than about differences in ideas, world views, and conceptions of humanity. Such debates are not easily settled. In writing *The Better Angels*, Pinker was opposing several schools of thought. One is a school of anthropology that Pinker calls "anthropologists for peace," which, he claims, is driven by an agenda: it wants to show that non-state* societies are peaceful. In contrast, Pinker does not want to prove that humans are either naturally peaceful or naturally violent. He paints a nuanced picture: humans can be either peaceful or violent, depending on their circumstances. It is, however, a crucial element of his argument that state-based societies help promote a decrease in violence. Responding to Pinker, these anthropologists assert that their aim is not ideological,* but empirical.*[6]

Another example of a hard-to-resolve debate is the one between Pinker and John Gray. In Gray's opinion, Pinker underestimates the violent events of the twentieth century, including Nazism* and Stalinism* (the political philosophy of Joseph Stalin,* leader of the communist Soviet Union* from the mid-1920s to 1953). He believes that Pinker's vision of the future is determined by his blind faith in science and lacks a deeper understanding of human nature. Gray's view is that "peace and freedom alternate with war and tyranny ... Instead of becoming ever stronger and more widely spread, civilization remains inherently fragile and regularly succumbs to barbarism."[7] Pinker replies by pointing out the ideological disagreement between them: "As a part of his [Gray's] campaign against reason, science and Enlightenment humanism, he insists that the strivings of humanity over the centuries have left us no better off."[8] His response to Gray's challenge is to highlight his statistical evidence that shows a decline in violence.

## NOTES

1   Jean Decety and Jason M. Cowell, "The Complex Relation Between Morality and Empathy," *Trends in Cognitive Sciences* 18, no. 7 (2014): 337–9.

2   Timothy Kohler et al., "The Better Angels of Their Nature: Declining Violence Through Time Among Prehispanic Farmers of the Pueblo Southwest," *American Antiquity* 79, no. 3 (2014): 444–64.

3   Steven Pinker, "Now For The Good News: Things Really Are Getting Better," *Guardian*, September 11, 2015, accessed December 19, 2015, http://www.theguardian.com/commentisfree/2015/sep/11/news-isis-syria-headlines-violence-steven-pinker.

4   Steven Pinker, *The Better Angels of Our Nature: Why Violence Has Declined* (London: Penguin, 2011), 377.

5   Steven Pinker, *The Blank Slate: the Modern Denial of Human Nature* (London: Penguin, 2002), 36.

6   Geoffrey Benjamin et al., "Violence: Finding Peace," *Science* 338, no. 6105 (2012): 327.

7   John Gray, "Steven Pinker is wrong about violence and war," *Guardian*, March 13, 2015, accessed December 30, 2015, http://www.theguardian.com/books/2015/mar/13/john-gray-steven-pinker-wrong-violence-war-declining.

8   Steven Pinker, "Guess what? More people are living in peace now. Just look at the numbers," *Guardian*, March 20, 2015, accessed December 30, 2015, http://www.theguardian.com/commentisfree/2015/mar/20/wars-john-gray-conflict-peace.

# MODULE 12
# WHERE NEXT?

## KEY POINTS

- *The Better Angels* is likely to remain a reference point for future studies on violence.

- Its impact is likely to be on research into the connections between the history and psychology* of violence.

- *The Better Angels* may also have an impact on the field of developmental psychology* (the study of the infant mind and how psychological faculties develop over time from birth to adulthood). Pinker suggests studying the evolution of violent psychology by looking at the context in which a person grows up.

### Potential

Steven Pinker's book *The Better Angels of Our Nature: How Violence Has Declined* has the potential to be at the center of future debates on the history, sociology* and psychology of violence. It introduces a bold thesis about violence and a clear methodology to support it.

Pinker's data shows that violence is declining. One of the book's strengths is that its arguments are founded on evidence. But new data may emerge to show that violence is increasing, contradicting Pinker's ideas. In an article published on September 11, 2015, Pinker looks at the new trends and claims that they still support his thesis: "The most concentrated forms of destruction our sorry species has dreamed up are world war and nuclear war, and we have extended our streak of avoiding them to 70 years. Wars between great powers, also hugely destructive, have been absent for almost as long—62 years."[1]

The book is largely descriptive: it presents historical trends and

> **❝** But headlines are a poor guide to history. People's sense of danger is warped by the availability of memorable examples—which is why we are more afraid of getting eaten by a shark than falling down the stairs, though the latter is likelier to kill us. Peaceful territories, no matter how numerous, don't make news, and people quickly forget the wars and atrocities of even the recent past. **❞**
>
> Steven Pinker, "Now For The Good News: Things Really Are Getting Better"

psychological explanations for violence. While Pinker does not attempt to give instructions as to how violence can be controlled and reduced, the connection he draws between psychology and society plays an important role in his overall argument. These ideas may have a particular impact on the educational sphere, and the ways in which pacifism* and cooperation can be taught.

### Future Directions

Although *The Better Angels* aims to connect psychology with history, the section of the book that dwells on psychology is shorter than Pinker's historical overview of violence. It is clear that more research is needed to discover how psychology is shaped by the historical context. Pinker mentions a model from cognitive anthropology* that argues that there are universal ways in which social relations are established and understood. These are the "relational models" developed by the American anthropologist Alan Fiske.* But the detail about how cognitive anthropology, psychology, and society are linked is not clear. There is work to be done on the evolutionary* aspects of conflict and of cooperation. This would give substance to the explanatory part of the book.

The book offers a starting point for both evolutionary psychologists* and developmental psychologists interested in discovering the origins of violence. Sociologists and historians interested in the book's major thesis are likely to look at the data it is based upon, and carefully analyze historical trends to confirm or refute it.

Another area in which Pinker's ideas may be applied is in the field of technology. Mark Zuckerberg,* the American founder of Facebook, has asked Pinker whether any data exists about the role of the Internet in reducing violence. Pinker has replied that new technologies play a role in the propagation of cosmopolitanism* (the belief that human beings form a single community) and that cosmopolitanism has a positive impact on violence.[2]

While Pinker might not have a group of disciples or students working on the topic of *The Better Angels*, he is surrounded by sympathetic colleagues, such as the Australian philosopher* Peter Singer* and the British evolutionary psychologist Richard Dawkins.* They are likely to carry on reflecting on the issues explored in the book.

## Summary

Violence is a central characteristic of human history and psychology. *The Better Angels* connects these two areas in a comprehensive study of the history of violence and its psychological roots. This ambitious book is one of Pinker's best sellers and the one that has sparked the most animated debate, both in the academic sphere and more widely. These debates are likely to continue.

Previous studies of violence have focused either on its history or on the psychology that underlies violent behavior, but few have brought these aspects together. In addition, most studies of violence have tended to view humanity in a polarized manner: either as originally good, but perverted by society, which has made it violent; or originally evil, and incapable of being changed by society. *The Better Angels* is not founded on either of these views. Pinker tries to show the ways in which nature and nurture* interact: while human biology is in many ways inflexible, society and culture can influence our behavior.

*The Better Angels* is an appealing book because it is positive about the future of humanity. Its thesis is supported by data and statistical analysis; it is not based on naïve optimism. The work is challenging, because its optimism contrasts with many people's intuitive view of the world as increasingly dangerous and threatening. It has become prominent, in part, because of its capacity to prompt a lively debate about one of the most central aspects of human nature: violence.

## NOTES

1   Steven Pinker, "Now For The Good News: Things Really Are Getting Better," *Guardian*, September 11, 2015, accessed December 30, 2015, http://www.theguardian.com/commentisfree/2015/sep/11/news-isis-syria-headlines-violence-steven-pinker.

2   Mark Zuckerberg, "A Year of Books," Facebook, January 28, 2015, accessed December 30, 2015, https://www.facebook.com/ayearofbooks/posts/831583243554273.

# GLOSSARY

# GLOSSARY OF TERMS

**Anarchism:** a theory in political philosophy that promotes eliminating the state and establishing self-governing, free societies. There are many strands of anarchism but they are all identified by the rejection of institutionalized political power. One of the main anarchist thinkers was the Russian revolutionary Mikhail Bakunin.

**Anthropology:** the study of humans. It concerns the study of all aspects of humanity: biological, linguistic, social, and cultural. It belongs to the field of social science.

**Arab Spring:** a term used to describe a series of violent and nonviolent protests, demonstrations, and civil wars that started in Tunisia and swept through the Arab world in 2010. As a result of the Arab Spring, rulers were forced from power in Tunisia, Egypt, Libya, and Yemen.

**Archeology:** a discipline that studies human life and activity in the past by exploring artifacts, architecture, and cultural landscapes (a combination of natural and man-made works). It belongs to the field of social science.

**Atheism:** the position that there are no deities or gods.

**Biology:** a field of study that belongs to the natural sciences and is concerned with the exploration of living organisms: their development, structure, function, classification, and distribution.

***Charlie Hebdo* attack**: the killing and injury of the members of the French satirical weekly newspaper *Charlie Hebdo*. It was carried out on January 7, 2015 by two gunmen who declared they were members of an al-Qaeda branch in Yemen.

**Christianity:** a monotheistic Abrahamic religion whose major text is the New Testament. The core belief of Christianity is that Jesus Christ is the Messiah, the savior of humanity, and was foreseen in the Old Testament.

**Civilizing process:** a term used by Steven Pinker and borrowed from the German-born sociologist Norbert Elias. The term indicates a set of institutional changes that began during the Middle Ages, and had an impact on human psychology that helped lead to a reduction in human violence.

**Climate change:** long-lasting changes in weather patterns. Climate change is mostly measured by archeological evidence, temperature measurements, and changes in vegetal and animal presence.

**Cognition:** used in a restricted sense, this refers to the mental faculties involved in post-perceptual processing, such as memory, judgment, decision-making, and language. Used in a broader sense, cognition refers to all mental processes, including perception, memory, attention, language, decision-making, reasoning, judgment, and problem-solving.

**Cognitive anthropology:** an approach to the study of anthropology that draws on the aims and methods of cognitive science.

**Cognitive science:** the interdisciplinary study of the mind and brain. It draws on philosophy, psychology, neuroscience, artificial intelligence, linguistics, and anthropology. Its core hypothesis is that the mind and the brain are representational-computational devices, similar in some respects to computers, and that we can study them by using experimental methods.

**Cold War:** a period of political and military tension between the Western Bloc (the United States and its allies) and the Eastern Bloc (the Soviet Union and its allies) that lasted from 1947 to 1991. It is called "cold" because it never resulted in direct conflict between the United States and the Soviet Union, but was conducted in satellite countries and mostly concerned the relative distribution of power.

**Collectivist anarchism:** a political theory that argued for the abolition of the state, and for the tools and resources required for production to be collectively owned.

**Colonialism:** the exploitation and government of a territory by a power from another territory.

**Communism:** an economical and political doctrine that believes societies should be based on the joint ownership of the resources and tools required for production (the "means of production") and the absence of social and economic inequalities.

**Cosmopolitanism:** the belief that all human beings are citizens of a single community. According to Steven Pinker, cosmopolitanism is one of the cultural forces that can help to reduce violence.

**Criminology:** an interdisciplinary field of research concerned with the exploration, understanding, and prevention of criminal behavior in individuals and societies.

**Crusades:** a series of wars fought between the eleventh and the thirteenth centuries. The first Crusade took place in 1095 when an army of Western European Christians set out to fight against Muslim forces and reconquer the Holy Land (the region located between the River Jordan and the Mediterranean).

**Darwinism:** a set of ideas associated with the English naturalist Charles Darwin and his theory of evolution.

**Democracy:** a system of government in which the people freely elect their representatives.

**Developmental psychology:** the study of the infant mind and the development of psychological faculties over time from birth to adulthood.

**Domestic violence:** the use of physical and psychological violence in the context of a family or home, usually by a partner.

**Economics:** an academic discipline that studies economic systems— the production, trade, and consumption of goods (material and non-material, such as services).

**Empathy:** the capacity to understand the situation, experiences, and feelings of others from their perspective rather than one's own.

**Empirical:** this term is usually applied to knowledge. It indicates knowledge acquired through observation and experiments rather than through mere reflection and theorizing.

**Empiricism:** a philosophical school of thought according to which knowledge comes from experience and that there are no innate bodies of knowledge. Associated with the philosophers John Locke, David Hume, and Thomas Hobbes. Also present in psychology.

**Enlightenment:** an intellectual movement that appeared in the eighteenth century in Europe (and partially in the United States), characterized by the appeal to rationality and the defense of liberty, tolerance, and rights.

**Equity feminism:** equity feminists are mostly interested in legal equality (for example, women receiving the same salary as men for doing the same work) and are neutral on the issue of gender roles. Gender feminists have a broader outlook and are often associated with the idea that gender roles are a social construction.

**Ethnography:** the study of people's cultures, particularly by observing them from the inside.

**Eurozone:** the monetary union of 19 member states of the European Union (while there are 28 EU states in total, 9 are not part of the Eurozone). These states have adopted the euro as their shared currency.

**Evolution:** processes occurring by means of changes in the heritable traits in a given biological population over time and generations.

**Evolutionary psychology:** the study of human and nonhuman psychology from the perspective of modern evolutionary theory.

**Expanding circle:** a concept proposed by the Australian moral philosopher Peter Singer. Singer says there is a moral progress as our moral concerns extend to beings that are not closely related to us. This connects with Steven Pinker's discussion of empathy as one of the psychological mechanisms that reduces violence.

**Experimental psychology:** the study of the human mind and behavior via methods that aim for measurable results that have a degree of scientific accuracy.

**Fat-tailed distribution:** a statistical distribution phenomenon, in which the values deviate from the average and produce unexpected results.

**Feminism:** a movement whose goal is to achieve equal rights for women and, more generally, to advocate for women in society, politics, and culture.

**Gender:** a set of characteristics broadly related to the difference between masculinity and femininity. Gender differences are not only biological, unlike sex differences.

**Genetics:** a subfield of biology concerned with the study of genes and heredity in living beings.

**Genocide:** the systematic elimination of a group based on racial, ethnic, religious, cultural, or national features.

**Global warming:** a gradual increase in the average temperature of the earth due to human influence on the climate and environment.

**Humanism:** a set of rational principles in which supreme importance is placed on humanity rather than on religious or "divine" institutions or figures.

**Human rights:** the most general set of rights to which humans are entitled, simply by virtue of being human: for example, freedom from torture.

**Human Security Report Project:** a research project studying peace and conflict, based in Canada. Its aim is to examine long-term trends in violent conflicts.

**Hunter-gatherer societies:** societies that obtain their food from hunting and collecting.

**Ideology:** a system of norms, beliefs, and theories held by a group or by individuals.

**Inquisition:** an institution established by the Christian Church in the thirteenth century to ensure the purity of belief and religious practice. Later it was notorious for the use of torture in the extraction of confessions.

**Leviathan:** a mythical monster in the Old Testament. The expression was used by the English philosopher Thomas Hobbes to indicate an absolute sovereign.

**Linguistics:** a discipline concerned with the study of language and its different aspects.

**Marxism:** the study of capital and economics associated with the German political philosopher Karl Marx, who saw history as being driven by economic forces and characterized by a struggle between classes.

**Medieval:** relating to the Middle Ages (fifth to fifteenth century).

**Middle Ages:** a period of European history between the fifth century (the decline of the Western Roman Empire) and the fifteenth century (the beginning of the period of European history known as the Renaissance).

**Modernization:** the process whereby societies are transformed from pre-industrial, traditional, agrarian, and religious to fully industrial, urban, and secular.

**Moral philosophy:** inquiry into the nature of "right behavior" and ethics.

**Nativist:** in the context of psychology, a nativist thinker believes that certain things are "native" to the human mind—in other words, we are born with them.

**Natural selection:** the main mechanism of evolution via which individuals breed and survive thanks to differences in their phenotypes (set of visible traits). The idea was introduced by the British naturalist Charles Darwin in his book *On the Origin of Species* (1859).

**Nature and nurture:** sometimes "nature versus nurture," the phrase indicates the opposition between two forces that influence development: "nature" refers to innate, biological factors, while "nurture" indicates external, environmental (including cultural and social) factors.

**Nazism:** a political and ideological set of ideas associated with the Nazi Party of Germany in the 1930s and 1940s.

**Noble savage:** an expression that indicates a hypothetical indigenous person who has not been corrupted and perverted by civilization. The term comes from Dryden's play *The Conquest of Granada* (1672). Often used in relation to Rousseau's theory that the "state of nature," or the natural human state, is peaceful.

**Non-state societies:** societies living without a stable state or authority. Examples of non-state societies are bands, tribes, and chiefdoms. Such societies were more widespread in the pre-historic era (around 10,000 B.C.E.), but this is now a marginal way of living.

**Normative:** pertaining to norms and rules for guiding behavior.

**Pacifism:** the refusal to sanction war, violence, and militarism.

**Philosophy:** a systematic study of the most fundamental nature of reality.

**Policy analysis/analyst:** the study and evaluation of policies and programs and their implications, aimed at solving public problems; a political analyst is one who engages in this study.

**Political activism:** actions aimed at promoting political changes. An example is going on strike.

**Political science:** the study of politics and how governments or political institutions work and behave, from a wide range of perspectives.

**Prescriptive:** related to guidelines and rules aimed at reinforcing certain kinds of behaviors.

**Psychology:** the scientific study of the mind and the behavior of groups and individuals. Psychology explores how mental functions, such as perception, memory, and decision-making, work. The subject belongs to the social sciences. In a general sense, the terms "psychology" and "psychological" refer to the workings of the mind.

**Pugnacity:** the tendency to be aggressive or pugnacious.

**Scientific method:** a set of steps used in science to investigate the world. It involves the careful formulation of a hypothesis and methods for testing that hypothesis.

**Secular:** not connected to religion; exempt from religious rules.

**Sociology:** the study of society. Examples of topics studied by sociologists are religion, politics, and social class. One of the social sciences.

**Social sciences:** a wide field of academic investigation that includes anthropology, archaeology, demography, economics, history, human geography, international relations, law, linguistics, political science, pedagogy, and psychology.

**Soviet Union (1922–91):** a former federation of communist republics that occupied the northern half of Asia and part of Eastern Europe, and was ruled from Moscow. Created from the Russian Empire in the aftermath of the 1917 Russian Revolution, the Soviet Union was the largest country in the world. After World War II, it emerged as a superpower that rivaled the United States and, as such, was one of the two main players in the Cold War.

**Stalinism:** the political and economic ideas of the Soviet dictator Joseph Stalin (1878–1953), characterized by state violence and systematic persecution of political opponents.

**State of nature:** a concept in political philosophy that indicated the hypothetical lives of people before the rise of societies and states.

**Syrian conflict:** an ongoing conflict that started in 2011 in Syria. It began with demonstrations against the government of the Syrian president, Bashar al-Assad, with protesters demanding his resignation. It continues to this day.

**Terrorism:** acts aimed at provoking terror, often with the purpose of having a political impact.

**Testosterone:** a hormone present in both nonhuman and human animals that is secreted mostly by testicles in human males and, in minor quantities, by ovaries in human females. Usually associated with masculine traits.

**Totalitarian:** a system of government in which the government intercedes in the lives of its citizens and in which dissent is aggressively prohibited.

**Ukrainian conflict:** an ongoing conflict that started in 2013 in Donetsk, Ukraine, between pro- and anti-Russian groups. Donetsk is an area of Ukraine in which the majority of the population speaks Russian.

**UNESCO:** the United Nations Educational, Scientific, and Cultural Organization. Its purpose is to promote education, science, and culture in the world as a way of contributing to peace and security.

**Uppsala Conflict Data Project**: a program founded in the 1970s and hosted at the University of Uppsala, Sweden. Its aim is to collect data on violent conflicts around the world.

**Women's rights:** rights aimed at promoting women's equality with men.

**World War:** a war involving most of the world's countries. The term refers to two events of the twentieth century: World War I (1914–18) and World War II (1939–45).

# PEOPLE MENTIONED IN THE TEXT

**Mikhail Bakunin (1814–76)** was a Russian revolutionary thinker, best known as one of the founders of the anarchist movement.

**Franz Boas (1858–1942)** was a German American thinker, considered one of the founders of modern anthropology. He taught at Columbia University where he established a school. One of his major texts is The Mind of Primitive Men, published in 1911.

**Noam Chomsky (b. 1928)** is an American linguist, cognitive scientist, and political activist. Professor emeritus at MIT, he is best known for his theory of "generative grammar." Steven Pinker helped bring his ideas on language to the broader public.

**Gregory Clark (b. 1957)** is an economic historian who specializes in the wealth of nations.

**Roger Cohen (b. 1955)** is an English journalist who writes for the New York Times and the International New York Times.

**Auguste Comte (1798–1857)** was a French philosopher and one of the founders of positivism, a philosophical movement based on the idea that all knowledge should be modeled on the example of scientific knowledge. He is considered one of the founders of sociology.

**Leda Cosmides (b. 1957)** is an American psychologist, best known as one of the founders of evolutionary psychology.

**John Crawfurd (1783–1868)** was a Scottish diplomat whose work anticipated ethnological studies.

**Martin Daly (b. 1944)** is a Canadian evolutionary psychologist.

**Charles Darwin (1809–82)** was an English naturalist, best known for his groundbreaking work on the theory of evolution in On the Origin of Species (1859).

**Richard Dawkins (b. 1941)** is a British ethologist (someone engaged in the study of animal behavior) and evolutionary psychologist, currently an emeritus fellow of New College in Oxford. He is best known for his 1976 book The Selfish Gene, which presents a gene-centered theory of evolution.

**Martin Dempsey (b. 1952)** is a United States army general who was the 18th chairman of the Joint Chiefs of Staff.

**David Deutsch (b. 1953)** is a British physicist at Oxford University; he also writes about creativity and the history of knowledge.

**Jared Diamond (b. 1937)** is an American scientist and professor of geography at the University of California, working in anthropology and evolutionary biology, among other fields.

**Norbert Elias (1897–1990)** was a German British sociologist, author of The Civilizing Process (published in German in 1939 and translated into English in 1969). This book examines how manners have changed over time and how these changes have had an impact on human psychology.

**Alan Fiske (b. 1947)** is an American anthropologist at the University of California who works on the anthropology and psychology of human relationships. He is best known for his theory of "social relational models."

**Bill Gates (b. 1955)** is an American entrepreneur, computer programmer, and philanthropist, best known as the cofounder of software company Microsoft.

**Joshua Goldstein (b. 1952)** is an American professor emeritus of international relations at the American University in Washington, DC; he specializes in war and society.

**Rebecca Goldstein (b. 1950)** is an American novelist, best known for her novel The Mind–Body Problem. She is Steven Pinker's third wife.

**John Gray (b. 1948)** is an English political philosopher and frequent contributor to newspapers such as the Guardian and the Times Literary Supplement. His most famous books are Straw Dogs: Thoughts on Humans and Other Animals (2003) and Black Mass: Apocalyptic Religion and the Death of Utopia (2007), in which he expresses a pessimistic outlook on humanity.

**Ted Robert Gurr (b. 1936)** is an American political scientist working on issues concerning political conflict. He is now professor emeritus at the University of Maryland.

**Ranald D. Hansen (d. 2014)** was a professor of psychology at Oakland University, specializing in the evolutionary psychology of violence and sexuality.

**Thomas Hobbes (1588–1679)** was an English philosopher who worked on a variety of topics, but is now best known for his political philosophy. His most famous book is Leviathan (1651).

**David Hume (1711–76)** was a Scottish philosopher and one of the major figures of the empiricist and skeptic tradition. His best-known work is A Treatise of Human Nature (1739–40).

**Robert Jervis (b. 1940)** is a professor of international affairs at Columbia University.

**Immanuel Kant (1724–1804)** was a German philosopher who worked on all areas of knowledge. His three Critiques are some of the most important works in the history of philosophy.

**Elizabeth Kolbert (b. 1961)** is an American journalist and contributor to the New Yorker.

**Stephen Kosslyn (b. 1948)** is an American psychologist and neuroscientist, best known for his work on mental imagery and information processing. He was Steven Pinker's advisor at Harvard University.

**Osama bin Mohammed bin Awad bin Laden (Osama bin Laden) (1957–2011)** was the founder of the terrorist group al-Qaeda and one of the instigators of the September 11, 2001 attacks on the United States of America.

**Jeff Lewis** is a professor of media and cultural studies at the RMIT University in Melbourne, Australia who has produced influential work on violence and terrorism.

**Abraham Lincoln (1809–65)** was the 16th president of the United States, in office during the American Civil War and assassinated just after the war ended.

**John Locke (1632–1704)** was an English philosopher in the empiricist tradition, mostly known for his conception of the mind and for his political philosophy.

**John Stuart Mill (1806–73)** was a British philosopher, economist, and political thinker and one of the main representatives of utilitarianism. His principal works were On Liberty and Utilitarianism.

**Robert Muchembled (b. 1944)** is a French historian who specializes in the history of violence; he is also interested in the history of sexuality. In 2011 he published the English translation of his book A History of Violence: From the End of the Middle Ages to the Present.

**Lewis Fry Richardson (1881–1953)** was an English mathematician, best known for his work on meteorology. He was one of the first thinkers to apply mathematical and statistical techniques to the study of the causes of wars and conflicts.

**Adam Roberts (b. 1940)** is an English professor of international relations at Oxford University, best known for his work on international security, organization, law, and civil resistance.

**Jean-Jacques Rousseau (1712–78)** was a French philosopher and Enlightenment thinker, best known for his work on political philosophy, human nature, and education.

**Rudolph Rummel (1932–2014)** was a historian of violence, who specialized in genocides. He invented the term "democide" to talk about systematic murder by governmental forces.

**Todd K. Shackelford (b. 1971)** is an American evolutionary psychologist and professor at Oakland University.

**Peter Singer (b. 1946)** is an Australian-born philosopher and professor of bioethics at Princeton University. He specializes in moral philosophy and ethics and is best known for his work on animal rights.

**Joseph Stalin (1878–1953)** was dictator of the Soviet Union, ruling as general secretary of the Communist Party from 1924 through to his death in 1953. Stalin's policies included forced collectivization of agriculture and forced industrialization—often at terrible human cost—and terrorization and purges of his enemies

**Nassim Nicholas Taleb (b. 1960)** is a Lebanese American statistician who specializes in studying randomness and probability. He is famous for his book The Black Swan.

**Bradley Alfred Thayer** is an associate professor of political science at the University of Minnesota Duluth. He wrote Darwin and International Relations: On the Evolutionary Origins of War and Ethnic Conflict (2004).

**John Tooby (b. 1952)** is an American anthropologist, best known for his work as an evolutionary psychologist, alongside his wife Leda Cosmides.

**Margo Wilson (1942–2009)** was a Canadian evolutionary psychologist, best known for her work on homicide and violence risk.

**Mark Zuckerberg (b. 1984)** is an American Internet entrepreneur, best known for being the founder of Facebook.

# WORKS CITED

# WORKS CITED

Benjamin, Geoffrey, Robert K. Dentan, Charles MacDonald, Kirk M. Endicott, Otto Steinmayer, and Barbara S. Nowak. "Violence: Finding Peace." *Science* 338, no. 6105 (2012): 327.

Clark, Gregory. *A Farewell to Alms: A Brief Economic History of the World*. Princeton, NJ: Princeton University Press, 2008.

Cohen, Roger. "A Climate of Fear." *New York Times*, October 27, 2011. Accessed December 22, 2015. http://www.nytimes.com/2014/10/28/opinion/roger-cohen-a-climate-of-fear.html.

Daly, Martin, and Margo Wilson. *Homicide*. New Brunswick, NJ: Transaction Publishers, 1988.

Decety, Jean, and Jason M. Cowell. "The Complex Relation between Morality and Empathy." *Trends in Cognitive Sciences* 18, no. 7 (2014): 337–9.

Deutsch, David. *The Beginning of Infinity: Explanations That Transform the World*. London: Penguin, 2011.

Dugdale, John. "Richard Dawkins Named World's Top Thinker in Poll." *Guardian*, April 23, 2013. Accessed December 22, 2015. http://www.theguardian.com/books/booksblog/2013/apr/25/richard-dawkins-named-top-thinker.

Elias, Norbert. *The Civilizing Process*. Translated by Edmund Jephcott. New York: Pantheon Books, 1982.

Ellingson, Terry Jay. *The Myth of the Noble Savage*. Berkeley: University of California Press, 2001.

Gates, Bill. "The Better Angels of Our Nature: Why Violence Has Declined." *Gatesnotes*, June 12, 2012. Accessed December 22, 2015. http://www.gatesnotes.com/Books/The-Better-Angels-of-Our-Nature.

Gleditsch, Nils Petter, Steven Pinker, Bradley A. Thayer, Jack S. Levy, and William R. Thompson. "The Forum: The Decline of War." *International Studies Review* 15, no. 3 (2013): 396–419.

Goldstein, Joshua S. *Winning the War on War: The Decline of Armed Conflict Worldwide*. New York: Dutton/Plume (Penguin), 2011.

Gray, John. *Straw Dogs: Thoughts on Humans and Other Animals*. London: Granta, 2004.

———. "Delusions of Peace." *Prospect* 21 (October 2011).

———. "John Gray: Steven Pinker Is Wrong about Violence and War."

*Guardian*, March 15, 2015. Accessed December 22, 2015. http://www.theguardian.com/books/2015/mar/13/john-gray-steven-pinker-wrong-violence-war-declining.

Hobbes, Thomas. *Leviathan*. Oxford: Clarendon Press, 2012 (1651).

Jervis, Robert. "Pinker the Prophet." *National Interest*, Nov–Dec 2011. Accessed December 22, 2015. http://nationalinterest.org/bookreview/pinker-the-prophet-6072.

Kim, Nam C. "Angels, Illusions, Hydras, and Chimeras: Violence and Humanity." *Reviews in Anthropology* 41, no. 4 (2012): 239–72.

Kohler, Timothy, Scott Ortman, Katie Grundtisch, Carly Fitzpatrick, and Sarah Cole. "The Better Angels of Their Nature: Declining Violence through Time among Prehispanic Farmers of the Pueblo Southwest." *American Antiquity* 79, no. 3 (July 1, 2014): 444–64. Accessed December 22, 2015. doi:10.7183/0002–7316.79.3.444.

Kolbert, Elizabeth. "Peace in Our Time: Steven Pinker's History of Violence." *The New Yorker*, October 3, 2011. Accessed December 30, 2015. http://www.newyorker.com/magazine/2011/10/03/peace-in-our-time-elizabeth-kolbert.

Kosslyn, Stephen M., Steven Pinker, George E. Smith, and Steven P. Schwartz. "On the Demystification of Mental Imagery." *Behavioral and Brain Sciences* 2, no. 4 (1979): 535–81.

LaFree, Gary, Karise Curtis, and David McDowall. "How Effective Are Our 'The Better Angels'? Assessing Country-Level Declines in Homicide since 1950." *European Journal of Criminology* 12, no. 4 (2015): 482–504.

Muchembled, Robert. *A History of Violence: From the end of the Middle Ages to the Present*. Cambridge: Polity Press, 2012.

Mueller, John. "War Has Almost Ceased to Exist: An Assessment." *Political Science Quarterly* 124, no. 2 (2009): 297–321.

Paulson, Steve. "Proud Atheists." *Salon*, October 15, 2007. Accessed December 22, 2015. http://www.salon.com/2007/10/15/pinker_goldstein/.

Pinker, Steven. *How the Mind Works*. New York: Norton, 1997.

———. "All About Evil." *New York Times*, October 29, 2000. Accessed December 22, 2015. http://www.nytimes.com/2000/10/29/books/all-about-evil.html.

———. *The Blank Slate: The Modern Denial of Human Nature*. London: Penguin, 2003.

———. *The Stuff of Thought: Language as a Window into Human Nature*. London: Penguin, 2007.

———. "The Moral Instinct." *New York Times*, January 13, 2008. Accessed December 22, 2015. http://www.nytimes.com/2008/01/13/magazine/13Psychology-t.html?pagewanted=all&_r=0.

———. *The Better Angels of Our Nature: The Decline of Violence in History and Its Causes*. London: Penguin, 2011.

———. "Decline of Violence: Taming the Devil within Us." *Nature* 478, no. 7369 (2011): 309–11.

———. *The Sense of Style: The Thinking Person's Guide to Writing in the 21st Century*. London: Penguin, 2014.

———. "Steven Pinker: By the Book." *New York Times: The Sunday Book Review*, September 25, 2014. Accessed December 22, 2015. http://www.nytimes.com/2014/09/28/books/review/steven-pinker-by-the-book.html.

———. "Graphic Evidence: Steven Pinker's Optimism on Trial." *Guardian*, September 11, 2015. Accessed December 22, 2015. http://www.theguardian.com/commentisfree/ng-interactive/2015/sep/11/graphic-evidence-steven-pinkers-optimism-on-trial.

———. "Now for the Good News: Things Really Are Getting Better." *Guardian*, September 11, 2015. Accessed December 29, 2015. http://www.theguardian.com/commentisfree/2015/sep/11/news-isis-syria-headlines-violence-steven-pinker

———. "Frequently Asked Questions about *The Better Angels of Our Nature: Why Violence Has Declined*." Steven Pinker: Department of Psychology, Harvard University. Accessed December 22, 2015. http://stevenpinker.com/pages/frequently-asked-questions-about-better-angels-our-nature-why-violence-has-declined.

———. "Has the Decline of Violence Reversed Since *The Better Angels of Our Nature* Was Written?" Accessed December 22, 2015. http://stevenpinker.com/files/pinker/files/has_the_decline_of_violence_reversed_since_the_better_angels_of_our_nature_was_written.pdf.

———. "Response to the Book Review Symposium: Steven Pinker, *The Better Angels of Our Nature*." *Sociology* 49, no.4 (2015): NP3–NP8.

———. *Words and Rules: The Ingredients of Language.* New York: Basic Books, 2015.

Pinker, Steven, and Elizabeth Spelke. "The Science of Gender and Science. Pinker vs. Spelke." *Edge: The Third Culture*, May 16, 2005. Accessed December 22, 2015. http://edge.org/3rd_culture/debate05/debate05_index.html.

Ray, Larry, Lea John, Rose Hilary, and Bhatt Chetan. "Book Review Symposium: Steven Pinker, *The Better Angels of Our Nature: A History of Violence and*

*Humanity.*" *Sociology* 47, no. 6 (2013): 1224–32.

Richardson, Lewis Fry. *Statistics of Deadly Quarrels*. Edited by Quincy Wright and C. C. Lienau. Pittsburgh: Boxwood Press, 1960.

Roberts, Adam. "The Long Peace Getting Longer." *Survival* 54, no. 1 (2012): 175–84.

Rousseau, Jean-Jacques. *Discourse on the Origin of Inequality*. Translated by Franklin Philip. Oxford: Oxford's World Classics, 2009 (1755).

Rummel, Rudolph J. *Death by Government.* New Brunswick, NJ: Transaction Publishers, 1997.

Schmidt, Bettina, and Ingo Schröder. *Anthropology of Violence and Conflict*. New York: Routledge/Psychology Press, 2001.

Shackelford, Todd Kennedy, and Ranald D. Hansen. *The Evolution of Violence*. New York: Springer Verlag, 2014.

Singer, Peter. *The Expanding Circle*. Oxford: Clarendon Press, 1981.

———. "Is Violence History?" *New York Times*, October 6, 2011. Accessed December 22, 2015. http://www.nytimes.com/2011/10/09/books/review/the-better-angels-of-our-nature-by-steven-pinker-book-review.html.

Taleb, Nassim Nicholas. Facebook entry, August 11, 2003. Accessed December 22, 2015. https://www.facebook.com/permalink.php?story_fbid=10151641931853375&id=13012333374

———. "Fat Tails, Model Uncertainty and the Law of Very Large Numbers." Accessed December 22, 2015. http://exploredoc.com/doc/4907575/how-large-the-n%3F—nassim-nicholas-taleb.

———. *The "Long Peace" Is a Statistical Illusion*. Accessed December 22, 2015. http://www.fooledbyrandomness.com/longpeace.pdf.

Tooby, John, and Leda Cosmides. "Groups in Mind: The Coalitional Roots of War and Morality." In *Human Morality and Sociality: Evolutionary and Comparative Perspectives*, edited by Henrik Hogh-Olesen, 91–234. New York: Palgrave Macmillan, 2010.

Viskontas, Indre, and Chris Mooney. "Steven Pinker on Violence." *Skeptical Inquirer* 37, no. 4 (August 2013). Accessed December 22, 2015. http://www.csicop.org/si/show/steven_pinker_on_violence/.

Zuckerberg, Mark. "A Year of Books." January 28, 2015, accessed December 30, 2015, https://www.facebook.com/ayearofbooks/posts/831583243554273.

# THE MACAT LIBRARY
# BY DISCIPLINE

## AFRICANA STUDIES

Chinua Achebe's *An Image of Africa: Racism in Conrad's Heart of Darkness*
W. E. B. Du Bois's *The Souls of Black Folk*
Zora Neale Huston's *Characteristics of Negro Expression*
Martin Luther King Jr's *Why We Can't Wait*
Toni Morrison's *Playing in the Dark: Whiteness in the American Literary Imagination*

## ANTHROPOLOGY

Arjun Appadurai's *Modernity at Large: Cultural Dimensions of Globalisation*
Philippe Ariès's *Centuries of Childhood*
Franz Boas's *Race, Language and Culture*
Kim Chan & Renée Mauborgne's *Blue Ocean Strategy*
Jared Diamond's *Guns, Germs & Steel: the Fate of Human Societies*
Jared Diamond's *Collapse: How Societies Choose to Fail or Survive*
E. E. Evans-Pritchard's *Witchcraft, Oracles and Magic Among the Azande*
James Ferguson's *The Anti-Politics Machine*
Clifford Geertz's *The Interpretation of Cultures*
David Graeber's *Debt: the First 5000 Years*
Karen Ho's *Liquidated: An Ethnography of Wall Street*
Geert Hofstede's *Culture's Consequences: Comparing Values, Behaviors, Institutes and Organizations across Nations*
Claude Lévi-Strauss's *Structural Anthropology*
Jay Macleod's *Ain't No Makin' It: Aspirations and Attainment in a Low-Income Neighborhood*
Saba Mahmood's *The Politics of Piety: The Islamic Revival and the Feminist Subject*
Marcel Mauss's *The Gift*

## BUSINESS

Jean Lave & Etienne Wenger's *Situated Learning*
Theodore Levitt's *Marketing Myopia*
Burton G. Malkiel's *A Random Walk Down Wall Street*
Douglas McGregor's *The Human Side of Enterprise*
Michael Porter's *Competitive Strategy: Creating and Sustaining Superior Performance*
John Kotter's *Leading Change*
C. K. Prahalad & Gary Hamel's *The Core Competence of the Corporation*

## CRIMINOLOGY

Michelle Alexander's *The New Jim Crow: Mass Incarceration in the Age of Colorblindness*
Michael R. Gottfredson & Travis Hirschi's *A General Theory of Crime*
Richard Herrnstein & Charles A. Murray's *The Bell Curve: Intelligence and Class Structure in American Life*
Elizabeth Loftus's *Eyewitness Testimony*
Jay Macleod's *Ain't No Makin' It: Aspirations and Attainment in a Low-Income Neighborhood*
Philip Zimbardo's *The Lucifer Effect*

## ECONOMICS

Janet Abu-Lughod's *Before European Hegemony*
Ha-Joon Chang's *Kicking Away the Ladder*
David Brion Davis's *The Problem of Slavery in the Age of Revolution*
Milton Friedman's *The Role of Monetary Policy*
Milton Friedman's *Capitalism and Freedom*
David Graeber's *Debt: the First 5000 Years*
Friedrich Hayek's *The Road to Serfdom*
Karen Ho's *Liquidated: An Ethnography of Wall Street*

John Maynard Keynes's *The General Theory of Employment, Interest and Money*
Charles P. Kindleberger's *Manias, Panics and Crashes*
Robert Lucas's *Why Doesn't Capital Flow from Rich to Poor Countries?*
Burton G. Malkiel's *A Random Walk Down Wall Street*
Thomas Robert Malthus's *An Essay on the Principle of Population*
Karl Marx's *Capital*
Thomas Piketty's *Capital in the Twenty-First Century*
Amartya Sen's *Development as Freedom*
Adam Smith's *The Wealth of Nations*
Nassim Nicholas Taleb's *The Black Swan: The Impact of the Highly Improbable*
Amos Tversky's & Daniel Kahneman's *Judgment under Uncertainty: Heuristics and Biases*
Mahbub Ul Haq's *Reflections on Human Development*
Max Weber's *The Protestant Ethic and the Spirit of Capitalism*

### FEMINISM AND GENDER STUDIES

Judith Butler's *Gender Trouble*
Simone De Beauvoir's *The Second Sex*
Michel Foucault's *History of Sexuality*
Betty Friedan's *The Feminine Mystique*
Saba Mahmood's *The Politics of Piety: The Islamic Revival and the Feminist Subject*
Joan Wallach Scott's *Gender and the Politics of History*
Mary Wollstonecraft's *A Vindication of the Rights of Women*
Virginia Woolf's *A Room of One's Own*

### GEOGRAPHY

The Brundtland Report's *Our Common Future*
Rachel Carson's *Silent Spring*
Charles Darwin's *On the Origin of Species*
James Ferguson's *The Anti-Politics Machine*
Jane Jacobs's *The Death and Life of Great American Cities*
James Lovelock's *Gaia: A New Look at Life on Earth*
Amartya Sen's *Development as Freedom*
Mathis Wackernagel & William Rees's *Our Ecological Footprint*

### HISTORY

Janet Abu-Lughod's *Before European Hegemony*
Benedict Anderson's *Imagined Communities*
Bernard Bailyn's *The Ideological Origins of the American Revolution*
Hanna Batatu's *The Old Social Classes And The Revolutionary Movements Of Iraq*
Christopher Browning's *Ordinary Men: Reserve Police Batallion 101 and the Final Solution in Poland*
Edmund Burke's *Reflections on the Revolution in France*
William Cronon's *Nature's Metropolis: Chicago And The Great West*
Alfred W. Crosby's *The Columbian Exchange*
Hamid Dabashi's *Iran: A People Interrupted*
David Brion Davis's *The Problem of Slavery in the Age of Revolution*
Nathalie Zemon Davis's *The Return of Martin Guerre*
Jared Diamond's *Guns, Germs & Steel: the Fate of Human Societies*
Frank Dikotter's *Mao's Great Famine*
John W Dower's *War Without Mercy: Race And Power In The Pacific War*
W. E. B. Du Bois's *The Souls of Black Folk*
Richard J. Evans's *In Defence of History*
Lucien Febvre's *The Problem of Unbelief in the 16th Century*
Sheila Fitzpatrick's *Everyday Stalinism*

Eric Foner's *Reconstruction: America's Unfinished Revolution, 1863-1877*
Michel Foucault's *Discipline and Punish*
Michel Foucault's *History of Sexuality*
Francis Fukuyama's *The End of History and the Last Man*
John Lewis Gaddis's *We Now Know: Rethinking Cold War History*
Ernest Gellner's *Nations and Nationalism*
Eugene Genovese's *Roll, Jordan, Roll: The World the Slaves Made*
Carlo Ginzburg's *The Night Battles*
Daniel Goldhagen's *Hitler's Willing Executioners*
Jack Goldstone's *Revolution and Rebellion in the Early Modern World*
Antonio Gramsci's *The Prison Notebooks*
Alexander Hamilton, John Jay & James Madison's *The Federalist Papers*
Christopher Hill's *The World Turned Upside Down*
Carole Hillenbrand's *The Crusades: Islamic Perspectives*
Thomas Hobbes's *Leviathan*
Eric Hobsbawm's *The Age Of Revolution*
John A. Hobson's *Imperialism: A Study*
Albert Hourani's *History of the Arab Peoples*
Samuel P. Huntington's *The Clash of Civilizations and the Remaking of World Order*
C. L. R. James's *The Black Jacobins*
Tony Judt's *Postwar: A History of Europe Since 1945*
Ernst Kantorowicz's *The King's Two Bodies: A Study in Medieval Political Theology*
Paul Kennedy's *The Rise and Fall of the Great Powers*
Ian Kershaw's *The "Hitler Myth": Image and Reality in the Third Reich*
John Maynard Keynes's *The General Theory of Employment, Interest and Money*
Charles P. Kindleberger's *Manias, Panics and Crashes*
Martin Luther King Jr's *Why We Can't Wait*
Henry Kissinger's *World Order: Reflections on the Character of Nations and the Course of History*
Thomas Kuhn's *The Structure of Scientific Revolutions*
Georges Lefebvre's *The Coming of the French Revolution*
John Locke's *Two Treatises of Government*
Niccolò Machiavelli's *The Prince*
Thomas Robert Malthus's *An Essay on the Principle of Population*
Mahmood Mamdani's *Citizen and Subject: Contemporary Africa And The Legacy Of Late Colonialism*
Karl Marx's *Capital*
Stanley Milgram's *Obedience to Authority*
John Stuart Mill's *On Liberty*
Thomas Paine's *Common Sense*
Thomas Paine's *Rights of Man*
Geoffrey Parker's *Global Crisis: War, Climate Change and Catastrophe in the Seventeenth Century*
Jonathan Riley-Smith's *The First Crusade and the Idea of Crusading*
Jean-Jacques Rousseau's *The Social Contract*
Joan Wallach Scott's *Gender and the Politics of History*
Theda Skocpol's *States and Social Revolutions*
Adam Smith's *The Wealth of Nations*
Timothy Snyder's *Bloodlands: Europe Between Hitler and Stalin*
Sun Tzu's *The Art of War*
Keith Thomas's *Religion and the Decline of Magic*
Thucydides's *The History of the Peloponnesian War*
Frederick Jackson Turner's *The Significance of the Frontier in American History*
Odd Arne Westad's *The Global Cold War: Third World Interventions And The Making Of Our Times*

## LITERATURE

Chinua Achebe's *An Image of Africa: Racism in Conrad's Heart of Darkness*
Roland Barthes's *Mythologies*
Homi K. Bhabha's *The Location of Culture*
Judith Butler's *Gender Trouble*
Simone De Beauvoir's *The Second Sex*
Ferdinand De Saussure's *Course in General Linguistics*
T. S. Eliot's *The Sacred Wood: Essays on Poetry and Criticism*
Zora Neale Huston's *Characteristics of Negro Expression*
Toni Morrison's *Playing in the Dark: Whiteness in the American Literary Imagination*
Edward Said's *Orientalism*
Gayatri Chakravorty Spivak's *Can the Subaltern Speak?*
Mary Wollstonecraft's *A Vindication of the Rights of Women*
Virginia Woolf's *A Room of One's Own*

## PHILOSOPHY

Elizabeth Anscombe's *Modern Moral Philosophy*
Hannah Arendt's *The Human Condition*
Aristotle's *Metaphysics*
Aristotle's *Nicomachean Ethics*
Edmund Gettier's *Is Justified True Belief Knowledge?*
Georg Wilhelm Friedrich Hegel's *Phenomenology of Spirit*
David Hume's *Dialogues Concerning Natural Religion*
David Hume's *The Enquiry for Human Understanding*
Immanuel Kant's *Religion within the Boundaries of Mere Reason*
Immanuel Kant's *Critique of Pure Reason*
Søren Kierkegaard's *The Sickness Unto Death*
Søren Kierkegaard's *Fear and Trembling*
C. S. Lewis's *The Abolition of Man*
Alasdair MacIntyre's *After Virtue*
Marcus Aurelius's *Meditations*
Friedrich Nietzsche's *On the Genealogy of Morality*
Friedrich Nietzsche's *Beyond Good and Evil*
Plato's *Republic*
Plato's *Symposium*
Jean-Jacques Rousseau's *The Social Contract*
Gilbert Ryle's *The Concept of Mind*
Baruch Spinoza's *Ethics*
Sun Tzu's *The Art of War*
Ludwig Wittgenstein's *Philosophical Investigations*

## POLITICS

Benedict Anderson's *Imagined Communities*
Aristotle's *Politics*
Bernard Bailyn's *The Ideological Origins of the American Revolution*
Edmund Burke's *Reflections on the Revolution in France*
John C. Calhoun's *A Disquisition on Government*
Ha-Joon Chang's *Kicking Away the Ladder*
Hamid Dabashi's *Iran: A People Interrupted*
Hamid Dabashi's *Theology of Discontent: The Ideological Foundation of the Islamic Revolution in Iran*
Robert Dahl's *Democracy and its Critics*
Robert Dahl's *Who Governs?*
David Brion Davis's *The Problem of Slavery in the Age of Revolution*

Alexis De Tocqueville's *Democracy in America*
James Ferguson's *The Anti-Politics Machine*
Frank Dikotter's *Mao's Great Famine*
Sheila Fitzpatrick's *Everyday Stalinism*
Eric Foner's *Reconstruction: America's Unfinished Revolution, 1863-1877*
Milton Friedman's *Capitalism and Freedom*
Francis Fukuyama's *The End of History and the Last Man*
John Lewis Gaddis's *We Now Know: Rethinking Cold War History*
Ernest Gellner's *Nations and Nationalism*
David Graeber's *Debt: the First 5000 Years*
Antonio Gramsci's *The Prison Notebooks*
Alexander Hamilton, John Jay & James Madison's *The Federalist Papers*
Friedrich Hayek's *The Road to Serfdom*
Christopher Hill's *The World Turned Upside Down*
Thomas Hobbes's *Leviathan*
John A. Hobson's *Imperialism: A Study*
Samuel P. Huntington's *The Clash of Civilizations and the Remaking of World Order*
Tony Judt's *Postwar: A History of Europe Since 1945*
David C. Kang's *China Rising: Peace, Power and Order in East Asia*
Paul Kennedy's *The Rise and Fall of Great Powers*
Robert Keohane's *After Hegemony*
Martin Luther King Jr.'s *Why We Can't Wait*
Henry Kissinger's *World Order: Reflections on the Character of Nations and the Course of History*
John Locke's *Two Treatises of Government*
Niccolò Machiavelli's *The Prince*
Thomas Robert Malthus's *An Essay on the Principle of Population*
Mahmood Mamdani's *Citizen and Subject: Contemporary Africa And The Legacy Of Late Colonialism*
Karl Marx's *Capital*
John Stuart Mill's *On Liberty*
John Stuart Mill's *Utilitarianism*
Hans Morgenthau's *Politics Among Nations*
Thomas Paine's *Common Sense*
Thomas Paine's *Rights of Man*
Thomas Piketty's *Capital in the Twenty-First Century*
Robert D. Putman's *Bowling Alone*
John Rawls's *Theory of Justice*
Jean-Jacques Rousseau's *The Social Contract*
Theda Skocpol's *States and Social Revolutions*
Adam Smith's *The Wealth of Nations*
Sun Tzu's *The Art of War*
Henry David Thoreau's *Civil Disobedience*
Thucydides's *The History of the Peloponnesian War*
Kenneth Waltz's *Theory of International Politics*
Max Weber's *Politics as a Vocation*
Odd Arne Westad's *The Global Cold War: Third World Interventions And The Making Of Our Times*

## POSTCOLONIAL STUDIES

Roland Barthes's *Mythologies*
Frantz Fanon's *Black Skin, White Masks*
Homi K. Bhabha's *The Location of Culture*
Gustavo Gutiérrez's *A Theology of Liberation*
Edward Said's *Orientalism*
Gayatri Chakravorty Spivak's *Can the Subaltern Speak?*

## PSYCHOLOGY

Gordon Allport's *The Nature of Prejudice*
Alan Baddeley & Graham Hitch's *Aggression: A Social Learning Analysis*
Albert Bandura's *Aggression: A Social Learning Analysis*
Leon Festinger's *A Theory of Cognitive Dissonance*
Sigmund Freud's *The Interpretation of Dreams*
Betty Friedan's *The Feminine Mystique*
Michael R. Gottfredson & Travis Hirschi's *A General Theory of Crime*
Eric Hoffer's *The True Believer: Thoughts on the Nature of Mass Movements*
William James's *Principles of Psychology*
Elizabeth Loftus's *Eyewitness Testimony*
A. H. Maslow's *A Theory of Human Motivation*
Stanley Milgram's *Obedience to Authority*
Steven Pinker's *The Better Angels of Our Nature*
Oliver Sacks's *The Man Who Mistook His Wife For a Hat*
Richard Thaler & Cass Sunstein's *Nudge: Improving Decisions About Health, Wealth and Happiness*
Amos Tversky's *Judgment under Uncertainty: Heuristics and Biases*
Philip Zimbardo's *The Lucifer Effect*

## SCIENCE

Rachel Carson's *Silent Spring*
William Cronon's *Nature's Metropolis: Chicago And The Great West*
Alfred W. Crosby's *The Columbian Exchange*
Charles Darwin's *On the Origin of Species*
Richard Dawkin's *The Selfish Gene*
Thomas Kuhn's *The Structure of Scientific Revolutions*
Geoffrey Parker's *Global Crisis: War, Climate Change and Catastrophe in the Seventeenth Century*
Mathis Wackernagel & William Rees's *Our Ecological Footprint*

## SOCIOLOGY

Michelle Alexander's *The New Jim Crow: Mass Incarceration in the Age of Colorblindness*
Gordon Allport's *The Nature of Prejudice*
Albert Bandura's *Aggression: A Social Learning Analysis*
Hanna Batatu's *The Old Social Classes And The Revolutionary Movements Of Iraq*
Ha-Joon Chang's *Kicking Away the Ladder*
W. E. B. Du Bois's *The Souls of Black Folk*
Émile Durkheim's *On Suicide*
Frantz Fanon's *Black Skin, White Masks*
Frantz Fanon's *The Wretched of the Earth*
Eric Foner's *Reconstruction: America's Unfinished Revolution, 1863-1877*
Eugene Genovese's *Roll, Jordan, Roll: The World the Slaves Made*
Jack Goldstone's *Revolution and Rebellion in the Early Modern World*
Antonio Gramsci's *The Prison Notebooks*
Richard Hermnstein & Charles A Murray's *The Bell Curve: Intelligence and Class Structure in American Life*
Eric Hoffer's *The True Believer: Thoughts on the Nature of Mass Movements*
Jane Jacobs's *The Death and Life of Great American Cities*
Robert Lucas's *Why Doesn't Capital Flow from Rich to Poor Countries?*
Jay Macleod's *Ain't No Makin' It: Aspirations and Attainment in a Low Income Neighborhood*
Elaine May's *Homeward Bound: American Families in the Cold War Era*
Douglas McGregor's *The Human Side of Enterprise*
C. Wright Mills's *The Sociological Imagination*

Thomas Piketty's *Capital in the Twenty-First Century*
Robert D. Putman's *Bowling Alone*
David Riesman's *The Lonely Crowd: A Study of the Changing American Character*
Edward Said's *Orientalism*
Joan Wallach Scott's *Gender and the Politics of History*
Theda Skocpol's *States and Social Revolutions*
Max Weber's *The Protestant Ethic and the Spirit of Capitalism*

## THEOLOGY

Augustine's *Confessions*
Benedict's *Rule of St Benedict*
Gustavo Gutiérrez's *A Theology of Liberation*
Carole Hillenbrand's *The Crusades: Islamic Perspectives*
David Hume's *Dialogues Concerning Natural Religion*
Immanuel Kant's *Religion within the Boundaries of Mere Reason*
Ernst Kantorowicz's *The King's Two Bodies: A Study in Medieval Political Theology*
Søren Kierkegaard's *The Sickness Unto Death*
C. S. Lewis's *The Abolition of Man*
Saba Mahmood's *The Politics of Piety: The Islamic Revival and the Feminist Subject*
Baruch Spinoza's *Ethics*
Keith Thomas's *Religion and the Decline of Magic*

## COMING SOON

Chris Argyris's *The Individual and the Organisation*
Seyla Benhabib's *The Rights of Others*
Walter Benjamin's *The Work Of Art in the Age of Mechanical Reproduction*
John Berger's *Ways of Seeing*
Pierre Bourdieu's *Outline of a Theory of Practice*
Mary Douglas's *Purity and Danger*
Roland Dworkin's *Taking Rights Seriously*
James G. March's *Exploration and Exploitation in Organisational Learning*
Ikujiro Nonaka's *A Dynamic Theory of Organizational Knowledge Creation*
Griselda Pollock's *Vision and Difference*
Amartya Sen's *Inequality Re-Examined*
Susan Sontag's *On Photography*
Yasser Tabbaa's *The Transformation of Islamic Art*
Ludwig von Mises's *Theory of Money and Credit*

The Macat Library By Discipline

Printed in Great Britain
by Amazon

87551439R00061